WITH GELDOF
IN AFRICA

Confronting the famine crisis

D0317357

WITH GELDOF IN AFRICA

Confronting the famine crisis

by David Blundy of *The Sunday Times*
and Paul Vallely of *The Times*

Photographs by Frank Herrmann

A TIMES/Band Aid publication
TIMES BOOKS, LONDON

Designed by David Driver assisted by John Pym

Printed in Great Britain by
John Bartholomew & Son Ltd.
Bound by Charles Letts Ltd.
Colour separation and typesetting
by the Vantage Group.
Printed on Fineblade Smooth paper made by
Townsend Hook & Co Ltd. and provided by
Hale Paper Company Ltd.

Published in Great Britain by
Times Books Ltd.,
16 Golden Square,
London, W.1.

in association with The Band Aid Trust

ISBN 0 7230 0279 7

ACKNOWLEDGEMENTS

My thanks to Charles Wilson, the Editor of *The Times*, who gave
me the time to write this book, to his predecessor, the late Charles
Douglas-Home, who allowed me to spend most of 1985 in Africa
and took such an interest in the results, and to Heather and
Catherine who had to put up with such long absences. **PV**.

I wish to thank *The Sunday Times*, which funded my trip and gave
me time to write the book, the staff of Times Books for their help
and Samira Osman who thought of the idea **DB**.

Introduction

Everything was final. Everything dark.

Without squinting you could see the dim, but huge and perfect sphere of the sun through the clouds of soil, turned to dust and risen 30,000 feet into the hot and dry sky.

It was like watching the cold English sun through a dusty window on some late October afternoon. But this sun burned. It burned everything. It burned so hot it was burning the continent beneath my feet.

For all of my life I had wanted to stand in that place which for us represents the end of the earth.

Well, I stood, mute with shock and gazing like Cortez with wild surmise not on some vast new ocean but at a sea of sand that moved and tumbled, as rough as any sea I've known. It whined across empty streets. It kicked dust devils into the already brown and heavy sky. It whipped itself furiously into hot gales around the crumbling clay houses and shrieked its way through the ropes and tents of Timbuctoo.

I was standing not only at the end of the earth but at what seemed to me to be an end of the world.

The desert is an all-devouring rapacious thing. It is alive and, like a wild uncontrolled animal, while it is on the move it is not possible to approach it with anything but fear. It invades you. It rips your clothes, sandblasts your face, glues your mouth. It clogs your nose, it cakes and mats your eyes, it plugs your ears, it cuts your skin, it dries you out, it kills your land, it burns you. It destroys all until it buries you alive.

I stumbled through Africa. I staggered through the shattering insouciance of the capital cities. I see-sawed between the passive and sometimes criminally stupid rationale of the government administrators and the often patronizing whining of the "old hand" aid agency headquarters and on into the grinding despair and grief of the affected areas. We shuttled between war zone and desert, famine and refugees, pomp and degradation, reason and chaos, sublimity and absurdity.

We would retreat at the end of each country in total confusion but with blessed relief to the small plane that had carried us in computerized luxury to this version of the apocalypse. There we would sit in our world attempting to make sense of what we had just seen and gratefully left behind: the scale of the horror, the utter devastation, whole civilizations cleared, languages erased, buildings buried, mass exodus, war, brutality and an incomprehensible stupidity and cruelty. But it was too big.

Reacting to Africa and its whole mad evil, my mind would toss out absurdities to compensate for the horror overload: jokes and football songs and phone calls home at 35,000 feet.

But nothing we could invent would be as absurd for me as reality.

I understood that these countries were doing me great honour by the ceremonial and welcome they gave me. But I'd never viewed a guard of honour before, nor had any wish to. I felt ridiculous and a fake. I felt uncomfortable when groups of children would sing songs about me and at me. Not anticipating this kind of thing and never having had to deal with it before, I simply pretended I was someone I saw on the news—which I was, anyway. So I became confused still further. I understand that they were saying thank you through me to millions of people, but as the disparity between the ceremony and protocol and the real reason for being there became ever clearer I grew terse and impatient. But they were being kind and I was trying not to be rude.

Still it became an exercise of will to continue. An unremitting catalogue of misery, a marathon of figures to be assimilated, reports read, proposals listened to, meetings, meetings. My mind swam with the jargon: "rehabilitation", "long-term development", "displaced persons", "stimulate the rural economy", "depress the local market".

But indignation was only a short drive away. Down in the camps whole nations lay huddled, wasted and ill. What everyone in those meetings was talking about was nothing less than the African holocaust. What they were describing was the death and hunger, the humiliation and hurt of millions upon millions of people who need not suffer it. What the figures meant was the sum total of our disregard for each other. What they added up to was the cost of all this dying to us all.

In Chad alone there are over 300 separate languages, totally distinct from one another. Some of them have gone already. I never heard them but I miss them. In these ways the lights of human genius wink out.

This journey was not some jaunt into a personal heart of darkness nor was it a dilettante's voyeuristic dip into the pitiless pain and degradation of others. It was a trip to refocus my outrage.

In the boredom of administration, explanation and justification you begin to lose sight of the purpose and reason for your anger. Questioning and rationalization begin to replace impulse and action. Then it is essential to recharge the batteries of grief.

The learning process was beneficial, the visible achievement satisfying, the contacts and meetings worthwhile . . . but who cares?

I'm not thinking about those things tonight. I'm thinking of what I saw. What I saw was humanity laid bare, degraded and shamed by its own malignant hand.

Bob Geldof, November 1985.

Flight into famine

The executive jet cruised at 475 miles per hour 37,000 feet above the Western Sahara desert. The exact position was displayed by the onboard navigation computer on a television screen in the back of the plane. Since our take-off early that morning, a little pulsating blob had moved almost imperceptibly across a map of Europe and North Africa, tracking our course from Hatfield, the British Aerospace airport just outside London, across France, Spain and the Canary Islands. Now the blob was creeping south, across Morocco.

The BA 125 series 800 is what the manufacturers call the state of the art in executive jets. Two jet engines propel it off the runway with the force and trajectory of a fighter aircraft. The cockpit is a star wars extravaganza of television screens radiating a soft, green light. The two pilots spend much of their time tapping numbered codes into the computer terminal. The plane seats eight passengers. There are five armchairs that swivel and recline and three bench seats at the back which face a 19-inch television rigged up to a video tape recorder and a quadraphonic tape deck. There is a radio telephone, cabinets made of simulated walnut, a toilet with gilt trimmings and a mural of an alpine scene.

It is the ultimate Western status symbol, the product of the finest avionic technology, designed to carry the barons of industry aloft cocooned in the comforts of the board room.

On October 7th 1985 the BA 125 was on a very different mission and had never carried a more motley crew. It was flying towards the most unfortunate countries in the world, where millions aspire, not to status symbols, but to simply finding enough to eat.

Bob Geldof, lead singer of the Boomtown Rats and chairman of Band Aid, slumped in an armchair and swivelled, restlessly, to and fro. He was exhausted. The night before he had been at a charity performance of the play *Pravda* in London's West End and now he carried a crumpled cheque for £16,000, made out to Band Aid, in the back pocket of his jeans. His hair, lank and matted, hung down to his shoulders. There was a two-day growth of stubble on his chin and bags under his eyes. He wore an unpressed orange shirt and sneakers, only half laced, with a skull and crossbones motif on the ankle. A figure of almost studied scruffiness, he was more in keeping with the Bowery than the splendours of an executive jet.

He was sitting opposite Kevin Jenden,

the director of Band Aid, an architect by profession and a snappy dresser with a penchant for leather jeans and tailored shirts unbuttoned to reveal a flurry of chest hair and a gold medallion. Geldof was to point out, frequently, that he looked like the last act in a Las Vegas nightclub. There was a three-man flight crew, two pilots and Cyril James, the Welsh engineer who had to double up as steward, and six members of the press: a three-man team from the BBC, reporters from *The Times* and *The Sunday Times*, and *Sunday Times* photographer Frank Herrmann. "The travelling circus", as Geldof put it.

The plane's interior was a mess. Bags

Geldof and Kevin Jenden, Band Aid's director, outside the executive jet.

were piled in the aisle and squeezed behind the backs of seats. A BBC film camera, sound equipment, a tripod in a round black tube the size of a rocket launcher, and Geldof's own video camera for home movies, formed small mountains in the cabin. Bags, files and papers were piled four feet high in the toilet, which the BBC reporter, Chris Morris, had already converted into a makeshift study, where later he would crouch for hours writing his television scripts.

Up in the calm of the BA 125, lulled by the soft drone of the engines, Geldof flicked through the fat files of Band Aid country reports and copies of *Africa Confidential*, boning up, like a presidential candidate on a whistlestop election tour, on the next port of call. He sang a country and western song loudly and mournfully

until Jenden told him to shut up.

Geldof and Jenden are a good team. Crudely defined, Geldof provides the glamour and the moral fervour, Jenden looks after the day-to-day running of the organization. It is a team that was brought into being almost a year before this trip began, as a result of the sudden, brilliant idea which came to Geldof one evening after watching a four-minute film by BBC reporter Michael Buerk about the famine in Ethiopia. Buerk had been to two feeding centres at Mekele and Korem. There had been so little food and so many starving people that the camp organizers were forced to pick those who would live and those who would die. They built a low fence around the centre. The people on the inside got subsistence rations. Those on the outside got nothing. Buerk filmed the crowds gazing in over the fence. They had, effectively, been condemned to death.

It pricked the conscience of the world. While the majority merely bemoaned the hopeless plight of the Ethiopian people, Geldof was outraged and stung into action. He organized the Band Aid record which raised £8 million. Then came Live Aid, and the campaign exploded.

For Geldof and Jenden, who gave up full-time work in his architectural practice to work unpaid on organizing Band Aid, it was and still is a dizzying and exhausting experience, one they still can't quite believe. Geldof would be sitting in the Chelsea home of his girlfriend, Paula Yates, and Jenden in his house in Stoke Newington, when the phone would ring. It would be the US State Department in Washington, the United Nations in New York, or the European Parliament in Strasbourg.

Geldof and Jenden went, with initial trepidation, to meet the Congress and Senate of the United States in Washington DC. There Geldof was awarded a medal of honour by the US black caucus—the first time a white had received one. It is one official tribute, out of the many showered on him in recent months, that he really treasures.

"I thought, Christ, here we are in the most powerful city in the world," says Geldof. The awe did not last long. When Tip O'Neill, the Speaker of the House of Representatives and one of a handful of truly powerful politicians in America, discovered that Geldof was not only the legendary fund raiser but also Irish, he hugged him. "Bob, if there is anything you need, and I mean anything, Bob, then just let me know," said O'Neill. Congressmen formed a queue to shake Bob and Kevin firmly by the hand. "They didn't look at us of course," says Geldof. "They shook hands with their heads twisted round so they could smile at the television cameras." It dawned on Geldof that as a lobbyist in the corridors of power he was unbeatable.

Band Aid has grown enormously in financial and political power. It has unleashed a dam of contributions which have swollen the funds to more than £50 million. It has spawned dozens of projects: Fashion Aid, Visual Aid, Schools Aid, Sports Aid, Band Aid France, USA for Africa, and at least 30 others all around the developed world. A pair of carpet slippers Geldof wore in Sudan were sold in London to a Los Angeles restaurateur for £10,000. Geldof and Jenden have badgered companies for ships, trucks, landrovers and pumps. They have harangued governments and institutions and fought their way skilfully through the undergrowth of bureaucracy, the main obstacle in the aid jungle. Although it has grown to have the power and prestige of a major corporation,

it still exists on a skeleton volunteer staff. Band Aid has experts: a lawyer, an accountant, a shipping expert, and an anthropologist—Jenden's wife, who also works full-time for no pay. It can tap the knowledge of specialist development departments at Sussex and Reading Universities, the School of Oriental and African Studies and the Hospital for Tropical Health and Diseases in London, and Georgetown University in Washington DC. But an enormous burden of work lies on the shoulders of Jenden and Geldof. "I am, quite often, totally knackered," says Geldof.

And to his surprise he has become, in a year, one of the most famous people in the world. In Britain a magazine poll said that Geldof was the person most people would like to meet. In Australia another poll voted him the man in the world with the most credibility. The Australian Prime Minister, Bob Hawke, came 19th. Geldof enjoyed a modest fame in the late 70s with the Boomtown Rats. Quite how modest, though, became clear

on the plane. Only one of his ten companions owned a tape or record of the Boomtown Rats. Most of us had never even heard one of his songs. Tim Rex, the BBC soundman, thought he remembered one called "I Don't Like Mondays".

"Doesn't it go like this?" he said, humming tunelessly.

"No, it f. . .ing doesn't," said Geldof.

His reputation in the 70s is nothing compared to his image in 1985, a heady concoction somewhere between Mother Theresa and James Dean. He has a lot of star qualities. He is photogenic and articulate; he looks like a rock and roll star but can speak with the polysyllabic fluency of a pundit. He has the demagogue's flair for the buzz word and the emotional phrase. He is intelligent. He is very funny. He is a journalist's dream, everything a chat show host could wish for.

Geldof does not handle his new fame well. There would be problems for Frank Herrmann and for Bill Nicol, the BBC cameraman, who naturally wanted shots of Geldof with children in the feeding

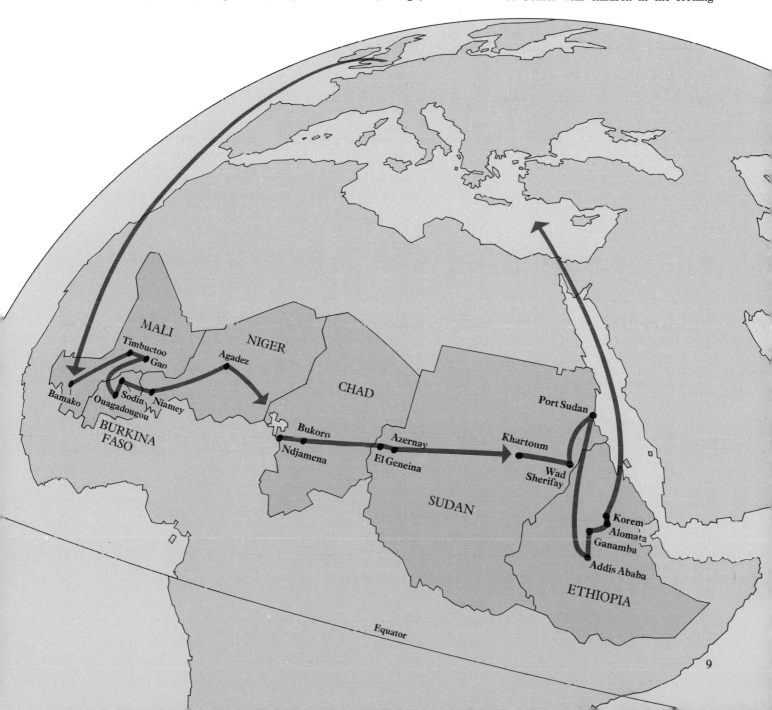

centres. Geldof refused. "That's the little black baby syndrome; it's patronizing and distasteful," he would say, dodging out of frame. Schedules would be hastily re-arranged or thrown away. Officials and diplomats would have their feelings bruised. The crisis would reach boiling point only three days into the trip.

Despite Band Aid's huge successes Geldof's thoughts were troubled as the pilots tapped the co-ordinates into the computer for the final leg of the trip towards Bamako, the capital of Mali. The main point of our journey to the Sahel region of Africa, those states on the southern flank of the Sahara which had been ravaged by drought and famine, was to draw attention to the plight of an area which had not fully impinged on the world's consciousness. Geldof and Jenden also wanted to look at how Band Aid money had been spent so far in Ethiopia and Sudan, and to see how best to spend around $1 million in the other four countries.

There were also deeper reasons. Geldof feared an onset of "compassion fatigue" in the general public and that the donors, often people who had never given to charity before, were becoming "famined out". Geldof had helped make compassion "hip", as he puts it, but there was a danger that it might have the life span of the average rock band. The aid experts like the Disasters Emergency Committee in London know the fickleness of the public, and know that contributions fluctuate wildly in direct relationship to the publicity famine receives. Geldof hoped to

bring the issue home once again through nightly broadcasts on the BBC, through articles in *The Times* and *The Sunday Times*.

And famine had become more complicated since the stark, dramatic images of the Buerk film. In many countries the immediate crisis was over. Thanks partly to governments, to agencies and to Band Aid, the food was reaching the majority of starving people in Africa. Rain, although often too little too late, had arrived in the Sahel. Some of the peasants had had a chance of gathering a harvest. The roots of the crisis had, however, barely been touched. If the famine victims had been saved from death, they were still in intensive care on the life support system of international aid. The scale of the tragedy was still staggering, as all of us would vividly see over the next two weeks. But now it had to be dealt with by long-term aid and development. How did you get this over to Band Aid donors?

"It's a problem," said Geldof. "Development is boring. I find it boring. How do you make a compressor pump interesting? I can't go on television and talk about deficits and surpluses and irrigation. People would turn off."

In the back of the plane Tim Rex switched on the video recorder and put on *Chariots of Fire*, one of the two video films in the library. The theme music boomed through the fuselage quadraphonically. In the front Geldof had launched into his first diatribe of the trip. Two weeks of sleeplessness and fatigue would not suppress

the flow of his scabrous rhetoric. "People shouldn't forget what this is; it's the African holocaust," he said. "You can't come up with specious f . . .ing arguments like Enoch Powell did in *The Guardian* this morning, saying Western aid is crypto-imperialism. If Powell confuses imperialism – which is a strong country exploiting a weak one – with helping people in need, then what price his much-vaunted intellectualism? Powell says we should let them go to hell in their own way. So we sit and let them die. It's shameful, shameful. Tim, will you turn that sodding music down? If one person is kept alive by anything Band Aid has done then it's worth it. In the face of things I've seen, like old ladies pulling off their wedding rings because they haven't got any money to give, I'm prepared to do something and I don't give a f . . . what people like Enoch Powell say about it."

Geldof was in a truculent mood. He was acutely aware that Band Aid had come in for its first volley of low-level sniping from the press. *Panorama*, the BBC programme, had criticized their truck project in Sudan. *The Daily Express* had accused them of being amateurs who did not know how to spend the money properly. The stories were not malicious, they were minor, and Geldof easily refuted

them. But he took the criticism to heart. His experiences with the music and popular press when he had been a struggling young Boomtown Rat had not, he said, been pleasant. "No offence to you, but the press are scum," he said.

"The papers get bored with calling you St Bob and all that rubbish so they start being snide. It's predictable. It's either sanctification or vilification." Geldof was right in a way, there was a backlash against Band Aid. Frankly it all seemed too good to be true. Was Geldof as sincere and

selfless as he appeared to be? Was the money being well spent? Could he avoid the bungling and in some cases the corruption that have been the downfall of well-meaning agencies? That was one of the reasons the press corps had joined him on the trip. "Snoop around all you want, lads," said Geldof.

The sanctification of Geldof is odd. There is little saintly about him. His speech is peppered with four-letter words which trip lightly and frequently off his tongue. In one ten-word sentence he

would use f . . . four times. This is how he speaks informally. His language is only slightly tempered in the presence of presidents, prime ministers and Catholic priests. After a while his use of the four-letter word becomes as inoffensive as a comma or a full stop. It is merely a manner of speech.

He also tells very long, very funny and very rude jokes and stories. One of them, about a donkey in Leeds, would take up almost an entire internal flight in Sudan. Immoderate language and a temper which explodes ferociously and often irrationally are perhaps his only visible vices. He has had his share of raucous nights out with the band, and his description of an evening in Zurich is hair-raising, but for a rock and roll star he is ascetic. He drinks alcohol, but moderately and rarely. He does not smoke or take drugs. He eats very little. He works compulsively and reads widely on an eclectic range of subjects, from history to music to politics and biographies. He dabbles in philosophy and got his phrase "moral imperative" from the German philosopher Kant. He is frugal with his own and especially Band Aid's money. This trip for example would cost Band Aid nothing. The plane was lent by British Aerospace. Its fuel and running costs were paid for by *The Sunday Times, The Times* and the BBC. Host governments picked up the hotel bills for Geldof and Jenden. His meals were paid for by whoever happened to be around at the time. It is

Geldof and BBC soundman Tim Rex look on as cameraman Bill Nicol captures in-flight scenes aboard the British Aerospace executive jet.

FACTORS IN THE FAMINE
THE SAHARA CREEPS SOUTHWARD

Desertification is the term which ecologists have coined to describe the process of degradation of the soil which turns productive farmland into sterile wilderness. Its major cause is thought to be a change in the climate on the edges of deserts, but it can also be brought about by years of over-cultivation, over-grazing and the cutting down of too many of the trees which fix the fertile top soil and prevent the desert winds from blowing it away.

The countries which are worst affected by famine in the north of Africa lie in the Sahel, the region of seasonal grasslands which runs along the belly of the Sahara. Once it provided, when the rains came in their intense local downpours, hundreds of areas of good grazing for the nomads who shifted their large herds of cattle and camels around the region in search of the new grass. In some areas the Sahel was even more productive.

"When I first came here 40 years ago it was all forest, full of wild animals: hyenas, lions, foxes and many birds," said one Niger Chieftain. From Mali to Sudan, local people tell similar stories.

CLIMATIC CHANGE

There is no consensus among the experts as to the ultimate cause of desertification. Some meteorologists claim that the climate of Africa is changing permanently. The odds of a drought lasting, as this one has, for 17 years are 125,000 to 1 according to Derek Winstanley at the US National Oceanic and Atmospheric Administration. He says that rainfall in the Sahel has, with fluctuations, been declining for 200 years. But others, including the World Meteorological Organization, believe that the drought is part of the normal climatic pattern. Either way, what is evident is that in a region as ecologically fragile as this, a very small change in overall rainfall, as little as five per cent, can produce drought.

Deserts, ecologists say, feed upon themselves and grow. The bare soil and stone reflect more solar radiation back into the atmosphere than do grass and trees. The increased reflectivity keeps the air hotter, disperses cloud and reduces rain. Without rain the grasses on the edges of the desert wither, a process exacerbated by over-grazing and the removal of trees which hold the soil for lesser vegetation. Without plants the wind throws more soil into the air. Increased evaporation lowers the moisture content of the earth and further suppresses rain.

Thus the Sahara silently creeps southwards. Today almost five million square miles, an area twice the size of India, are at risk from desertification in sub-Saharan Africa.

CASH CROPS

The prime human cause of desertification is over-cultivation of poor soils by farmers extending their planting into unsuitable areas. Three main factors cause this practice: increasingly governments and rich landowners are taking over more good land for the growth of cash crops and forcing subsistence farmers onto land which was previously considered marginal; Africa's rapidly increasing population demands more food; and as the poor land quickly becomes exhausted the peasants are forced onto even poorer land. Other causes include over-grazing of the uncultivated areas by nomads' animals, and the felling of trees for firewood or to create clearings for cultivation.

This human desertification is not limited to the fringes of the Sahara. It can happen anywhere where there are too many people taking more out of the land than nature can put back into it. This is the problem in the Ethiopian highlands, where farmers are now forced to plough hillsides so steep they have to rope themselves and their oxen to tree stumps to prevent them from falling into the deep ravines at the bottom.

The more the top soil is disturbed by ploughing and the natural vegetation stripped away in places like this, the more vulnerable it becomes to erosion by wind and flood. In the Sahel and Ethiopia rains, when they do come, are torrential and cause flashfloods which wash away the top soil. Then the farmers are forced onto even more marginal land. Thus the cycle of erosion has a ratchet effect. In the 1960s 5.2 million people were affected by such floods in the Sahel. In the 1970s that figure had risen to 15.4 million. In the 1980s it is higher still.

SOIL CONSERVATION

To the change in the weather there is no answer. To human desertification the obvious solution is to stop the over-working and halt the process with anti-erosion terraces and soil and water conservation projects. Some progress was made in this direction in Ethiopia. But the work is back-breaking and its effects are only long-term. Now, with another period of crisis upon them, peasants find it hard to sacrifice short-term benefits to the long-term good.

"You tell me not to cut down this tree for firewood. Alive, the tree will keep the desert at bay," said one Sudanese woman on a wood-gathering expedition. "Fine. But tell me this: What do I use to cook tomorrow's dinner for my five children?"

quite possible that Band Aid paid for not as much as a cup of tea during our two-week trip.

He likes to have a laugh. On the plane he was to play Trivial Pursuit compulsively. As the wheels rose into the undercarriage after take-off he would grab the boxes of questions and say in a public-school voice, "It's time for Trivers Purs." Geldof is very good at it but, to his irritation, not as good as Jenden.

There were no jokes or games as we began the gentle descent towards Mali. Geldof and Jenden rifled through the Mali files and they were grim reading: Mali is one of the five poorest countries in Africa; "Mali reports a deepening of its crisis as a result of deteriorating health, food supplies and transportation conditions," said a report from June '85; total population 8.1 million, total population affected by drought 1.2 million; ten per cent of national livestock dead because of famine. Even the recent rains had brought problems, washing away crops and villages.

As we crossed the Malian border the pulsating blob that charted our course dropped, almost symbolically, off the bottom of the screen and disappeared. The computer's map was designed to take the jet to the places executives go to: Europe, the Middle East and the northern fringes of Africa. Both the computer and Geldof were venturing into the unknown.

MALI
Early warnings

As we taxied across Bamako airport the digits of the onboard computer, which also gave the outside air temperature, began spinning upwards. It had been a brisk autumn morning in Hatfield. Now the numbers were moving through the 80s to settle at 94. It was evening in Mali and, by local standards, a pleasant, quite cool one. For us, as we left the airconditioned womb of the BA 125 for the first time in West Africa, it was a shock. In the hot, moist air, sweat began to trickle over the scalp and through the shirt. The feeling was to stay with us for the rest of the trip. Often it would be so bad that a little waterfall of sweat would trickle down Geldof's forehead and plop off the end of his nose, smudging ink on official documents.

There was a reception committee on the tarmac: Mr Sory Ba, from the Mali Ministry of Protocol, who wore a flowing blue robe, a bevy of officials, a member of the Red Cross League and the British Honorary Consul, Harvey Smith, who was pale and bearded. There were also insects, by the million. Geldof was scratching and

Right top Meeting aid workers. Kevin Jenden is on Geldof's right. *Right below* The first interview for Chris Morris of the BBC.

batting at them before we reached the terminal. Even on the tarmac of the airport there were huge, green grasshoppers, three inches long. Their hops were olympic. They landed with a thud on your back, head or shoulders. The locals ignored them. We were terrified. Geldof began to move around the airport reception room like a dancing dervish, trying to shake off a giant grasshopper which had landed and nested in his hair.

"There has been a plague of grasshoppers in Mali," said the Honorary Consul, in the VIP lounge. "They wiped out 90 per cent of the crop in Nara in northwest Mali." A French photographer who had just made a tour of Central Africa had more bad news: "Be very careful. It is the malaria season now and my friend is sick in hospital. You should see the hospital, my God. I have had dysentery. It was horrible. And be careful of the women, you know, the hookers. They are beautiful but they have AIDS." This later became a topic of intense, although purely academic, discussion in our group. Someone had read an article which said that more than 40 per cent of the prostitutes in Nairobi had AIDS antibodies. Someone else said AIDS could be contracted from tear drops. Geldof scared us all by saying that he had read that grasshoppers carry AIDS virus. "I swear I read that. I'm not having you on, honest," said Geldof. "I read it in a reputable magazine. It wasn't in some old rubbish like *The Times*." "I've never heard of anyone having it off with a grasshopper," said Jenden.

Inside the VIP lounge Geldof faced a more immediate problem, one that would dog him for a week. When the officials spoke to him Geldof could not understand anything they said. Mali and the next three countries we visited are francophone. People speak French and dozens of local languages. Neither Geldof nor Jenden could speak any of them. A mind-numbing ritual of translation from French into English and English into French, or even Malian dialect into French, into English, began. Every speech, meeting, reception and conversation, many of them ponderous in one language, would take twice as long.

Mr Sory Ba got up to make a speech of welcome. Geldof slumped lower in his chair, scratching furiously.

"Vous êtes Bob Geldof," said Ba.

"You are Bob Geldof," said the interpreter.

"Vous êtes célèbre dans tous les pays du monde et dans Mali."

"You are famous throughout the world and in Mali."

"Vous avez voyagé loin."

"You have come a long way."

"Vous êtes bien venu dans notre pays."

"You are welcome in our country."

"Nous espérons que vous aurez beaucoup d'épreuves agréables dans notre pays."

"We hope you have many pleasant experiences in our country."

"Right then," said Geldof, getting to his feet. "That's very nice. Thanks a lot then."

"D'accord. Vous êtes très gentille. Alors, merci beaucoup," said the interpreter.

We drove in buses over the River Niger, which is enormous, into Bamako's

Above Geldof haggling for cloth at the Pink Market, Bamako. *Right* Stall holders cleaning their teeth with twigs, Bamako market.

---

sleepy town centre. Dodgem cars raced around a tiny track put up in the main square by a French entrepreneur who was taking them on a tour of Africa. It was the biggest attraction in town. In the capital people have enough to eat and, by the standards of their countrymen in the desert and rural areas, they are well off. But even in Bamako many live in shacks without running water, sanitation or electricity. Their monthly income is what we, in the West, would spend on a modest lunch. An aid worker said that evening: "We pay our driver an above average salary in local currency. He is lucky. He has a job and dozens of people apply for the same job every week. But he keeps a wife, children, his wife's family, his own mother and father, cousins and people who have come from the country because there is no food. His children do odd jobs in the market to make some extra money. By our standards his life is a nightmare. Here he is one of the fortunate ones. Each day is a real struggle to survive. Don't forget this." It was a sobering thought.

For Geldof, Bamako was a long way from the stadium at Wembley where, last July, the trip was made possible. Then he had stood in front of the audiences watching simultaneously in London and Philadelphia while a further 1500 million people viewed the concert live as it was beamed to their televisions by satellite. It was watched by more people than any other event in history. Geldof himself was

Above For the Geldof family album.
Right Sizing it up for Band Aid money.
·The market garden project at Gao,
Mali. *Overleaf* Ladling out the food aid.
UNICEF feeding centre, Timbuctoo,
Mali.

awed. "I felt we had tapped in to some sort of global compassion. When I went on stage I realized for the first time the romance and hugeness of it all. People in China, New Caledonia and Khartoum were watching at that exact instant. I had not anticipated the emotional impact which is the single most important aspect of Live Aid. With this feeling anything was possible."

He raised more than £50 million for the famine in Africa that night. The euphoria did not last long, however. Geldof came down to earth. Spending that money in a way that would help people most directly would consume his energy for months to come.

Work began immediately at the L'Amitié hotel in Bamako. Jenden went to a meeting of local aid organizations to talk about details. Geldof went down to the hotel cafeteria to do what he likes best, getting his teeth stuck into a Western politician. This time the French Minister for Co-operation (with whom or what was not quite clear), who had been touring the former French West Africa. There is perhaps nothing in the world, except singing with the Boomtown Rats, that Geldof relishes more than attacking the European Economic Community. It raises him to flights of rhetoric, invective and sheer venom that have reduced sophisticated members of the European Parliament to a shocked silence. The EEC and any of its member countries represent for Geldof the epitome of wasteful bureaucracy, governmental bungling

and, Western arrogance. Or as Geldof put it: "It pisses me off."

Minister Nucci, a rugged, handsome man, evidently unaware of Geldof's predilections, summoned the correspondent from French radio to the table where he was sitting. "Switch on your tape recorder. Quick, switch it on," said the Minister. He basked in the television lights. Geldof listened politely as the Minister explained how the famine in Mali was not as bad as in Ethiopia because the French Government had anticipated the problem and had implemented plans to

fight desertification. Then Geldof went for the throat. "What I don't understand about you people in the EEC is why you don't open your grain silos and send it to where it's needed most. You can talk about your plans and your anticipation but you and your colleagues could stop starvation this week. There are people starving out there, Minister. It's such a waste. The EEC could be such a useful organization. You've got the money. That needs to be translated into will."

The tape recorder whirred and the Minister tried to regain some lost ground.

"I think you do not understand the issues of agricultural policy; it is a difficult and complicated subject," he said.

"It is not an agricultural problem, it's a moral problem, Minister," said Geldof. "Why did the EEC pay £10 million for a report on how to get rid of two million pounds of butter? Why did the Council of Ministers cut their overseas aid programme by £100 million last month?"

Nucci perspired gently, perhaps not only from the Mali heat. "I don't know about that," he said.

"I don't doubt the Minister's concern.

But the EEC has the huge amounts of money needed to do the job. What it lacks is the political will to spend it for effective change. This is the African holocaust." Game, set, match to Geldof.

The Minister fairly jogged out of the cafeteria to catch his plane to Paris. Geldof relaxed. He is not malicious. "He's a nice bloke, that Minister," he said. "It's a funny thing how all French politicians seem to look like Alain Delon." Geldof's moral fervour, although undoubtedly sincere, can be turned on and off with disquieting speed. His use of the grand

abstracts "moral imperative", "African holocaust", "a Marshall plan for Africa"—was to grow frankly tiresome during the trip, as he used them with the facility with which he employs the four-letter word.

Geldof in private is a good deal more pragmatic than Geldof on the nightly news. Upstairs in the bar at the L'Amitié Geldof sipped a beer, the band played a Frank Sinatra song, a line of prostitutes, looking pretty but potentially as dangerous as grasshoppers, sat on the bar stools. Geldof explained that he sees his

role as a PR man for famine relief. "I know I say crass things. But if I talked about the complications of aid and famine nobody would understand. OK, look, I know that if you build a well in a desert area then people come to it because there's water. Then they stay there and more people come. They bring cattle. The cattle overgraze the area immediately around the well. People step in the cattle shit, they go near the water, the water gets polluted. So you're back where you started. If I go on TV and say that then people will say, 'Well, what the f. . .. Why should I do anything?'" Geldof stokes the fires of his own outrage because he believes that sheer willpower and effort can have results. And it has made people give money, made governments change, however slightly, their policies.

People in Bamako that night were less bothered by such high moral issues. Word was out that a big celebrity was in town. Many got it slightly wrong. The band leader at the L'Amitié approached the press corps and asked if any of us was Bob Geldof.

"No," we said.

"That is a great pity," said the band leader. "I heard that he was coming here to put on a concert and I hoped that he would sing tonight with the band."

This would be a common misconception during the trip. Even government officials when they first met Geldof seemed to think he was about to burst into song.

All of us had been given a neatly typed three-page document called "The Visit of Mr Bob Geldof to Mali". A presidential candidate could not have wished for more. It contained a map of Bamako town centre and "useful telephone numbers", which included the office and home numbers of a doctor and the emergency department of the local hospital. It also contained the schedule. The first item on Tuesday, October 8th, was a "courtesy visit to His Excellency Ahmed Mohamed Ag Hamani, Minister of Sports, Arts and Culture." Geldof did not like the look of it.

"Why are we seeing him?" he asked the man from the Red Cross who had helped to organize the trip. "We're here to find out about famine. We're not making a state visit. Cut that out."

"I can't cut that out, he's a Minister. You've got to understand there's protocol involved here. I can't ring up a Minister and say, 'Good morning. Mr Geldof thinks meeting you is boring, so we've cut you out'."

"F. . .ing protocol," said Geldof.

At 8 am, according to schedule, he was ushered in to see Mr Hamani, who seemed about as keen on the visit as Geldof. It was the first confrontation on this trip with third-world ceremonial. The Minister, a refined but taciturn man, had a dark, small office. An air conditioner wheezed away against one wall, faltered, then stopped. The conversation took a similar course. Mr Hamani came from Timbuctoo. Why, someone asked, was Timbuctoo said to be

Above 'Geldof d'Afrique', slaking his thirst after the desert. *Right* Washing lettuce on the banks of the Niger at the market garden project at Gao in Mali.

such a mysterious place? Everyone had heard that, but nobody seemed to know quite why.

"If I told you why it is mysterious then it would not be mysterious," said the Minister. There was silence.

"Minister, do you know where I could go to hear some good music?" said Geldof.

The Minister thought for a long time.

"Yes," he said. "There is a festival of music being held in Mali in two months' time."

"Minister, I mean tonight," said Geldof.

The Minister looked blank and shook his head. The strangest meeting of his official career came swiftly to an end.

The serious business of the trip was scheduled for noon. Geldof and Jenden were there to spend a million US dollars, and the best way to do it, they decided, was to ask the experts, the aid workers based in Mali. There are a lot of them. The schedule listed: International Plan; CARE Mali; World Vision; Médecins Sans Frontières; Save the Children Fund (UK); Oxfam; AFVP; AETA; CECAMA; AMADE; AFRAM; ASF; AVN; CECI; CEPAZE; CIDR; CLCA; DED; EAA; EMI; Helvetas; LACIM; Six S; SECAMA; SUCO; Terre des Hommes (France); Terra Nova; VSF; World Relief; British Volunteers. From this point on conversations would be punctuated by initials, meaningless to all but the cognoscenti of aid.

Some of the aid agencies, like USAID, spend hundreds of millions of dollars and are huge, like corporations. Others are tiny and work on single agricultural projects in the savannah or the desert. They include learned experts on aid, men and women who have devoted a lifetime, with little financial reward, to helping the third world. There is a scattering of dewy-eyed young people, called aid groupies by the professionals, who are often more

hindrance than help. The aid workers form a distinct society in the African countries we visited, roaring around the dirt roads in their landrovers and Japanese land cruisers. They talk a separate aid dialect, full of strange expressions: "MSF says the interface with the NGOs is failing, and the ETA of the EAA and AFVP non-food shipments to the NGO HQ is delayed."

About 40 of them waited for Geldof under a tent in the yard of the LORCS (League of Red Cross Societies), subdued by the heat. Many later confessed they felt hostile towards Geldof when the meeting began. The feeling is understandable. They had been summoned away from their projects to meet a rock and roll singer who had dealt with famine for only a year, and part-time at that. One American said it peeved him. He and his colleagues had worked in Mali for more than four years. Although they were well paid by local standards they had been ignored by the media, and even the Malian Government treated them with suspicion and, sometimes, downright hostility.

And yet here was a musician arriving in a private jet, lauded by the local dignitaries, trailing television and newspaper journalists. "It is aid theatre," he said.

Geldof is aware of this. His opening remarks at this meeting, and all the others that followed, were aimed at soothing feelings and setting minds at rest. "Look, I don't know the best way to spend the money. I need you to tell me. All I ask is that you reach a consensus about the best way to do it."

The approach worked well. Although Geldof often has a hectoring tone and a schoolmaster's testiness at such meetings, he genuinely wants to know the problems and to get advice. The aid workers appreciated it. "He's not as arrogant as I first thought," said a nurse. "He's bright. He knows about aid and he's doing the right thing, going to the experts." This was fine in theory, but in practice Geldof's calls for consensus ran into trouble.

There was not even agreement among the agencies on the state of the famine in Mali. Some believed people were still dying in their thousands in the remote north. Others said the famine was over, leaving the problem of displaced people and long-term measures to repair the agriculture.

Even when they agreed on the problem, they disagreed about how to cope with it. Geldof and Jenden made an initial suggestion: use the Band Aid money to start a warehouse, a sort of central supermarket of aid, where the different agencies could collect, for example, cement, or compressors for pumps, or agricultural implements. Some agencies pointed out that they worked hundreds of miles from Bamako; there were no roads, and getting to the warehouse would be a major problem. Others thought individual agencies could handle their own supplies better than a central system.

One aid worker, an Englishman called

Steve Cobb, thought the meeting had missed the point. The problem of drought in Mali could not be solved by money, he said. "My project has money, it just lacks enough knowledge. Countries and agencies have poured $300 million a year into the Sahel region," said Cobb. "It has done very little good. There are two problems. One is the climate, and we can't do anything about that. The other is the Government, and nobody wants to do anything about it." Cobb's research project, which is two days from Bamako, one by road and one by boat, studies people who have been forced out of their nomadic way of life by drought. He believes that the Government's approach is wrong. "It encourages the nomads to go to feeding centres where they hope to get free food. During the 500-mile walk their last two donkeys die. They are dispirited. When they arrive they often find they can't get food and they are too weak to go back." He believes that nomadism is the best way to use 85 per cent of the land surface of Mali. "They should not be settled and the Government only wants them to be settled so that it can collect taxes which swell the ranks of civil servants. The nomads should go back to the old system of grazing and fishing which they have done expertly for 2000 years."

Cobb is not a popular man among the aid workers, partly because he challenges the established view and is not afraid to criticize the Government. He put the same points to the Duke of Edinburgh who visited his project in 1985. The Duke had a rotten trip. It was intensely hot and there were dust storms. He rattled around for

Above **A new mosque built by UNICEF at Gao, Mali, for settled Tuareg nomads. It demonstrates techniques for building without wood.** *Right* **Nomadic tribesmen in the settlement camp at Gao, Mali.**

two days in the front of Cobb's landrover. The Duke, who has definite views on land conservation in Africa, disagreed with Cobb at first. Later, in Geneva where he addressed a conference, he seemed, to Cobb at least, to swing round. Geldof was easier to convince. He too believes that governments are the key to famine crises, and the trip would provide ample evidence to support that view.

After two hours in the foetid tent, Geldof had had enough. The interpreter's voice grew hoarse and consensus seemed to melt away in the heat. "I'm off," said Geldof. "You talk about it among yourselves and then let me know what you decide."

Like schoolboys sneaking away from class, we all went to the Bamako market. It is made of castellated pink clay and is one of the most beautiful in Africa. Geldof likes markets. He hoisted his new video camera onto his shoulder, and became a tourist. For the people of Bamako market it was a bizarre sight: Geldof with his camera being filmed by Bill Nicol of the BBC, and both of them being photographed by Frank Herrmann.

After the heavy negotiations in the tent Geldof quickly got bogged down in another one with a mud cloth salesman. Geldof wanted to get his girlfriend Paula some mud cloth, which is black with pretty white designs made by masking

areas of the cloth with wet mud before dyeing it. "How much?" he said to the stall holder through an interpreter into a Malian dialect. "Four pounds [its equivalent in local currency]," said the stall holder. "I'll give you two," said Geldof. The stall holder rolled his eyes and clutched his heart. "OK look, I'll buy in bulk. I'll give you ten pounds for four." "Sixteen pounds," said the stall holder.

"Leave it to me," said Geldof. "We'll walk away as if we're not interested, then we'll wander back all casual like and then we'll have him." We walked away. Twenty minutes later we sauntered back. "OK," said Geldof. "Four of them for twelve pounds." "Sixteen pounds," said the stall holder. "OK, f . . . it. Give him sixteen. Christ!" said Geldof.

TIMBUCTOO
Engulfed by the desert

No-one would admit it, but there was a feeling of conspiracy in the air. Timbuctoo was not on the itinerary but it was a place we all wanted to visit. As usual it was Geldof who articulated everyone's unspoken thoughts.

"I'm buggered if I'm coming all this way and not going to Timbuctoo," he said. "Get this schedule altered."

"Good idea," said the television reporter, who was rather looking forward to ending his dispatch with "This is Chris Morris, BBC, in Timbuctoo".

HOW AFRICAN LEADERS MAKE THE FAMINE WORSE

For drought to turn into disaster it requires more than poor weather and ill luck. It also requires, among other things, short-sighted policies on the part of each African government.

Much of the blame for these lies with the situation the government inherited from its colonial masters. The Europeans often sited the capital city not in the best place from which to administer the country, but in the spot which gave greatest access to the outside world. In order to facilitate the easy transport of goods to Europe, the capital would be on the coast or as near to it as possible. (Hence N'Djamena in Chad, Niamey in Niger, Bamako in Mali are all in the extreme southwest corner of their vast countries.) There was no need to build up a network of towns in the colony; all trade could go straight from the countryside through the metropolis, thus creating a capital which was as much as eight times bigger than any other town in the country. Independence did little more than substitute for a white elite a black one which still looked to the West in every way. Even the expensive symbols of new African nationhood were Western in design: hotels, conference centres, dams and universities. To pay for it all the West gave sizeable loans to be repaid through the sale of cash crops like cotton, tobacco, cocoa, peanuts, sugar, tea, coffee and palm oil.

COLONIAL LEGACY

This is the colonial legacy: a capital out of touch with the country, rulers out of touch with the people, and a huge metropolis with an ever-increasing population and newly educated elite.

To find jobs for the university graduates and prevent them from becoming a disaffected opposition, the government bureaucracy has been expanded. In Mali, for example, one of the five poorest countries in the world, the essentially non-productive civil service is now, by a factor of ten, the largest employer. Mali has also been made the base for the Institut du Sahel, one of the many bodies spawned by the Comité Internationale de Lutte contre Sécheresse du Sahel (CILSS), the Sahel's version of the EEC set up to distribute bureaucratic largesse around its member states. Very often the civil servants actually act against the interests of the people. Drawn from the metropolitan elite, they often resent being stationed out in the provincial wilds. Sometimes the result is inefficiency, as in Niger where bureaucrats with no experience of stock-rearing were sent out to manage government ranches. In other cases it leads to corruption: civil servants in the town of Youvarou in Mali were recently caught registering the arrival of food aid and then immediately returning it to the capital for sale. Such practices are common throughout the Sahel.

PRICE FIXING

To find cheap food for the urban population, nationalized bodies like the Agricultural Marketing Corporation in Ethiopia have been established to buy food from farmers at low prices fixed by the government. There is little incentive for farmers to produce extra food at such poor prices—in Cameroon, for example, cocoa farmers in 1977 received only 18.8 per cent of the market price under this system, compared with 80.8 per cent in Brazil. The result is a harvest which is much smaller than the country is capable of producing. The US State Department claims that cereal production in Mali, Burkina Faso, Niger and Chad could be doubled if these fixed price systems were abolished and if existing irrigation projects were better managed. Most African rulers are aware of the problem. Some have taken limited steps to rectify it; in Mali in 1985 the fixed price on millet has been abolished, though it is maintained on rice. But on the whole governments prefer unhappy farmers out in the countryside to unhappy city dwellers who are much more likely to riot and overthrow the existing regime.

The governments have run into problems with their cash crops too. The world recession has upset the economic equation the Africans were handed on independence: in 1971 one Sahelian cow bought a barrel of oil, in 1981 it took nine cows.

In the two years 1980–82 alone, prices for cash crops fell 27 per cent, on top of the declines of the 1970s when Africa's share of the world coffee market dropped from 34 per cent to 23 per cent and its share of palm oil sales fell from 57 per cent to 29 per cent (largely because one company, Unilever, shifted its investments from West Africa to Malaysia).

NATIONAL DEBTS

At the same time costs have risen—oil prices, interest rates and the value of the US dollar (in which debt repayments are mainly made). Repayments which were 8.8 per cent of their income in 1973, were 10 years later 25 per cent. In a country like Niger (not the worst example) 40 billion francs of an annual budget of 86 billion goes in interest on its national debt. Burkina Faso has a higher per capita debt than Mexico or Brazil. In Sudan last year the interest alone on its $9000 million debt was more than its entire annual income.

The only solution has been to increase cash crop production. The result is that in 1984, the year of famine, Burkina Faso, Mali, Niger, Senegal and Chad gathered in a record cotton harvest of 154 million tons (compared with 23 million in 1967) while the Sahel also imported via food aid a record amount of cereals—1.77 million tons, compared with 0.2 million in the early 1960s.

The result has also been to force subsistence farmers, who produce more than 90 per cent of the food, off the good land and onto marginal land, thus increasing desertification. Unhappily much of the cash cropping has been done by speculators on a short-term basis, extracting quick profits and putting nothing back into the land.

Government policies to change the whole economic basis away from the capital and exports and towards self-sufficiency are at least being tried in Burkina Faso, but there is little sign of them elsewhere.

There was, interjected Jenden hastily, a very interesting project there that it would be good to have a look at.

"Yes, and we can get our passports stamped 'Timbuctoo'," said Geldof, now with undisguised schoolboy enthusiasm.

The next day the jet took off from Bamako and headed north.

For hundreds of years the very word Timbuctoo has been a synonym for the most remote place on earth, but today the little desert settlement faces a new kind of extremity. From the 12th century onwards this forbidden city has carried on an impenetrable existence at the far side of the world's largest desert, and at the heart of a kingdom as mysterious to the first European explorers as were the blue-veiled faces of the Tuareg nomads who appeared suddenly out of the sand dunes. But to these Berber peoples and the merchants for whom the place was the crossroads of the ancient caravan routes, Timbuctoo was a haven from the eternal unyielding harshness of the Sahara, a place of rich grazing for thousands of cattle and camels, a university town, a

Right top **Aid agency meeting.**
Right below **In Geldof's honour, dancers at a concert in Ouagadougou.**

revered centre of worship and a market place of both commercial and cultural exchange.

Circling the town in the jet it was clear that things are very different now. During the last two decades the desert has been reclaiming Timbuctoo. There has been a drought here for the past 17 years; for the last four of them it has been increasingly severe and this year the area has had only

CONSEIL OECUMENIQUE
DES EGLISES

SAVE THE CHILDREN
FUND - UK

OXFAM

IRIS

THE CHICKEN

AFRICARE

CAS
CATHWEL

half as much rain as in the previous parched year. The sands of the Sahara are moving south. Every year the encroachment has continued until now the desert has swept around the town and surrounded it entirely.

There was a party of aid workers and local dignitaries waiting on the tarmac to greet the Band Aid team. The town commissioner, a burly fellow in baggy military fatigues, came to attention with a smart salute and offered Geldof his hand.

"Have you the passports?" he asked, as though telling us we were entering a different country. In reality he was acknowledging the fact that virtually the only saleable commodity his barren territory now had to offer the outside world was the magical name which visitors so treasure in the pages of their passports. "Tombouctou," the locals call it, in deference to the language of their former colonial masters, the French. Just before the town, which is joined to the airport by the only stretch of tarmac road in hundreds of miles, our convoy of landrovers pulled up before a gigantic noticeboard which offered visitors both a "Bienvenu à Tombouctou" in French and a "Welcome to Timbuctoo" in English. The Band Aid party piled out for the obligatory photograph.

In the town the streets were full of the soft sand which is slowly swallowing the buildings. In the courtyards of the mud-walled houses it lay ankle deep. By the sides of the 16th-century Sankore mosque it was piled in little drifts. Only 20 years ago it was possible to arrive here by boat along a canal branching from the River Niger. The waterway even continued another 250 miles further north out into the Sahara — halfway towards the Taoudennit salt mines and a world unreached by modern values, a world where even today, it is said, slave labour is used to quarry the desert's only treasure. But of that part of the canal there remains no trace at all. These days even the mighty Niger itself dries: in former times 1500 cubic metres of water flowed every second over its vast river bed; in May 1985 that was reduced to a mere two cubic metres; in places upstream it now dries up completely for five months of the year. And the old canal into Timbuctoo is now just a shallow depression, its sides cracked and crumbled, with heaps of old rubbish on its bed. Among the blackened tin cans and piles of rotting vegetable matter, skinny donkeys grub for sustenance.

"God, the place is a dump," said Geldof, unconsciously echoing the sentiments of the first Europeans to arrive here. But unlike the British explorer Gordon Laing, said to be the first white man to enter Timbuctoo in 1826, who was murdered by his treacherous Tuareg guides, Geldof did at least survive to tell the tale.

Geldof and the Minister: Josephine Ouedraogo, Minister of Families and National Solidarity.

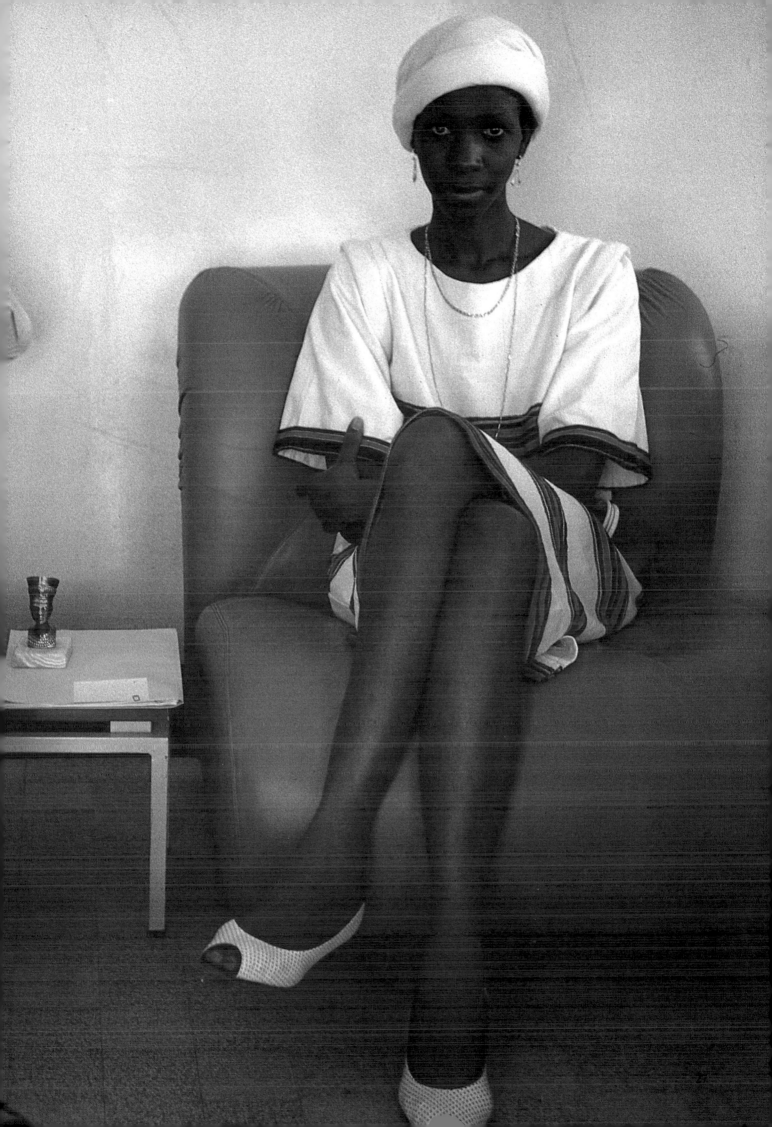

From the legendary name it is difficult for the visitor not to expect a city of some substance, or at the very least some ruined palace or other relic of a glorious past. In the Middle Ages it was said that the buildings of Timbuctoo were roofed with gold, but, if they ever were, the 16th-century invaders from Morocco or the greedy sands of the Sahara devoured them long ago.

Today all there is to see in Timbuctoo is a few grubby streets of low mud buildings in the French-colonial style and a market of a dozen or so poorly provisioned stalls which mock at the memory of one of the world's great trading centres. Most of the merchants who once ran the town have now abandoned it and moved south across the river to Dire. Of the great university of Sankore, which intellectually dominated Muslim culture in West Africa for 200 years, there remains little but a dusty bundle of manuscripts in the municipal museum. The ancient mosque is nothing more than a pyramid of mud and sticks which the traveller could be forgiven for thinking predated its older Egyptian counterparts by several centuries; to appreciate the achievement it represents you need to know that one of the great advances of the Mali civilization was the replacement of the simple mud wall with the invention of the mud brick.

"Is that it?" said a disbelieving Geldof. It was.

Ten miles outside the town is the symbol of a more recent civilization, a Belgian development project called the Ile de Paix. If there is any hope of stemming the inexorable tide of the desert as it sweeps southwards, it lies, Geldof was told, in projects like this. Here massive engine-

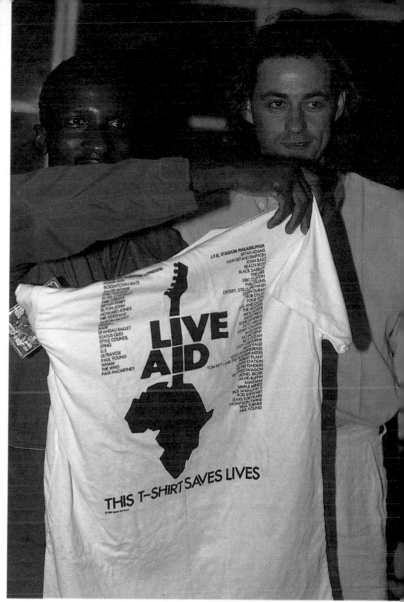

Above Captain Thomas Sankara, President of Burkina Faso, tells Geldof and Jenden that "running a country is like running a rock group", *Above right* Geldof gives Sankara a present. *Below* A reluctant Geldof performs with the Little Singers of the Raised Fist.

houses power huge Archimedes screws which drag more than 4000 gallons of water every second from the Niger and spread it through 30 miles of irrigation channels into a network of artificial rice paddies. They extend from the river bank out, like a green mist, towards the horizon. At their edges the sand lies grey and barren, a vivid demonstration of what little the land can offer without the assistance of agricultural technology.

"The desert has advanced more than 200 miles southwards in the ten years I have lived in Timbuctoo," said the

project's engineer, Eugene Van Camfort, a grizzled, weatherbeaten Belgian in late middle age. He was sceptical about the plans of the desk men in Bamako to stem the sands by drilling 35,000 wells in a line across the desert further north and then planting trees around them to fix the shifting sands.

"It's too expensive. What people have to face up to is that the climate here is undergoing a permanent change and we have lost the battle against the desert in the north. We have to give up on all that land. The only place the desert can be halted is

29

here at the river with schemes like this one."

It was getting very hot. When we had landed the jet's thermometer had registered 110 degrees F and still the intense white sun was rising in the cloudless sky. One of the local drivers looked with concern at his VIP guest whose head was bare to the sun. From his own head he unpeeled the long white linen band which makes up the traditional headgear of the region and wound it around Geldof's woolly locks.

Geldof grinned.

"How do I look? Lawrence of Arabia?" he said, striking a mock-heroic pose.

"More like Peter O'Toole, on a bad day," responded one of the more unkind members of the Band Aid party. But he had gone sufficiently native to inspire the local officials to ask him to join in the work of planting out the small rice seedlings.

"This is the bit I really hate. I'll look like a complete dick in the photos," said Geldof, bending ungraciously and scowling at the photographer. He fumbled in the watery soil while the eight-year-old boy placed alongside him as an exemplar pushed the little plants into position with speed, ease and a cheeky grin.

For a rock star Geldof has an extraordinarily ambivalent attitude to photographs. He is quite happy to be pictured looking silly in an Arab turban or raising his fingers at the camera in a gesture of abuse. Yet he has a deep dislike of appearing in a picture alongside one of the people Band Aid has set out to help.

"It is distasteful. It is patronizing. It is exploiting people. It is part of the black baby syndrome which I despise," he said

irritably. Eugene Van Camfort deftly changed the subject by bombarding Geldof with facts and figures about the Ile de Paix.

Geldof was clearly impressed with the scheme. "It costs $12,000 a hectare to set up this system which can then produce three tons of rice a year. A family of eight to ten needs two tons to survive, which leaves them with a ton to sell. From the profits they contribute to the maintenance of the irrigation equipment. So the beauty of it is that once the initial investment is made with Western aid money the scheme is self-financing," he repeated to his journalistic entourage.

"That's right," said the veteran Belgian engineer. "There has been very little rain here again this year, only 110 mm all season. There will be no harvest within 400 miles of here, except on this project."

But the Ile de Paix is just that, an island of peace, and a very small island in a vast sea of burning sand which has few equals for sheer inhospitability anywhere in the world. By its riverside edge live little groups of casual labourers who work in the planting season on the project. Once they were nomadic herders, but all their animals died in the great drought. Now these people are fettered to the banks of the Niger. The men work in the paddy fields. The women gather cooking fuel, fetch water and prepare the sticky porridge which is their staple food. The children, who in their former lives from the age of five had great responsibility as herders of the family cattle, now sit and watch the 30-foot-long cargo canoes sliding elegantly along the

Above Local cottage industry, baking bricks in the sun, Yatenga province, Burkina Faso. *Right* A starving man in a village without food or medicine. Geldof demands to know why. Bogoya, Burkina Faso.

mud-brown waters. But if there is little for them to do here, there is even less away from the project.

Between it and the town, Geldof came across another group of nomads, arbitrarily located in the middle of an unending wasteland of infertile grey dust. These were totally destitute, without even the labourer's pittance earned by the Ile de Paix families. The group, or "fraction" as such tribes are known in Mali, is only one of dozens which now cling to the fringes of Timbuctoo. For though the place is dying as a centre of commerce its population has, ironically, been doubled by the 20,000 nomads who have moved down from the unyielding desert to the outskirts of the unproductive town, where they are kept alive by a UNICEF feeding programme.

This was the first camp Bob Geldof was to see on his journey across Africa. The children were a sad spectacle as they clustered around the food tent and jostled for the high-energy food, which looked like a yellow semolina, as it was ladled into their empty bowls. It was not that they were desperately malnourished. Six months of international food aid had rectified that problem. "The depressing thing is that so little lies before them," said Geldof. "We have saved their lives, but what is the next step for them? The West can go on feeding them like this, but that is no long-term solution."

The problem of what ought to come next, after the food aid, confronted the Band Aid team even more starkly in Gao, another ancient caravan town further to the east. There free food was not just postponing the decisions on how to cope with the long-term problems, it was actually making the situation worse.

The massive graveyard on the edge of the town showed just how desperately food aid had been needed here in Mali earlier in 1985. The little cairns of stones that marked each human defeat in Gao's Muslim cemetery stretched on and on. The place had grown to five times its original size in the past nine months.

When Geldof and Jenden arrived there was plenty of food reaching Gao — at long last. The American marines were there, operating a US army ferry, a replacement for the local one which had broken down at the most crucial period and reduced people to ferrying the food aid from each 40-ton lorry across the broad river in dozens of tiny canoes. Soviet government technicians were there too, working on runway repairs for urgent aircraft deliveries. Here the frost of the Cold War had thawed to nothing more than friendly gin-drinking competitions between the two groups of workers. But such international concord came late for this landlocked country; only now, when thousands of Gao's 60,000 shanty-town refugees were dead, was the food aid actually arriving. The further consequences of that tardiness were most disturbing.

"Locally grown rice and millet sell here for about 120 francs a kilo. But what hope have local farmers of getting a fair price for their crop when plenty of US aid maize has found its way illegally onto the black market at 25 francs a kilo. There is too much food aid here, now," one angry aid worker from Euro-Action Acord told Geldof. It would destroy the farmers' ability to raise the cash to pay for seeds for next year's planting. It would also change the diet of the local people and build up a dependence upon a food which could not be grown in the area.

Free food had even brought about a halt to work on a local hospital, Belgian officials of the medical agency Médecins Sans Frontières told him.

"Local people had been building it for us at Menaka. We were paying them with food for their labour. Then two other agencies came along with all the free food which had just arrived. When they gave it out everybody just stopped working for us," said one dark-haired young doctor who cornered Geldof as the Band Aid chairman sat over a lunch of stringy chicken in a dingy Gao hotel. Another relief worker explained how the influx of free food was jeopardizing a long-term

The locals did not want Geldof to come into the village as their bowls were empty and they had nothing to offer him. Bogoya, Burkina Faso.

33

development project which involved giving revolving loans to unproductive farming co-operatives in the area so that they could establish mutually beneficial trading relationships with more successful co-ops in the productive southern regions of Mali. The free food was breaking the newly established links.

But it was the eager little children of that first camp outside Timbuctoo, sitting in a wilderness of creeping sand, with their hands outstretched towards an uncertain future, who most potently symbolized the colossal problems—human, economic and geographic—which beset the famine-stricken areas of Africa. And all the time that Saharan sun fixes them in its relentless gaze.

"God, I need a drink," said Geldof, mopping the sweat from his brow with the corner of his white turban. The Band Aid landrovers set out for the L'Azalai hotel. It stood on a mound at the edge of Timbuctoo, a building of orange-brown mud bricks which could once have been the colonial fort of the local French administrator or the home of the original Beau Geste. An archway led through the exterior wall into a quadrangle of ornate paths. Between the paths, bright pink flowers clung to the freshly watered ground by the shortest of stalks, as if they were afraid to grow too far from the source of the vital moisture. But, for all the lavish attention of its gardener, the L'Azalai too was a place of the past.

Geldof slumped into a low armchair in the hotel foyer. Behind him a faded blackboard offered champagne at a price which would have seemed extortionate in even a West End restaurant, though it was probably not unreasonable for merchandise which must have made the last stage of the journey from France on the back of a camel. Geldof sat with his leg over the arm of the chair and drank warm Fanta orange. His limbs felt drained by the heat and beneath his ludicrously lopsided white turban his face was drawn. Mali was the first of six countries and Africa was already beginning to take its toll.

"What about postcards. We have to send postcards from Timbuctoo," he said with sudden animation. But the kiosk in the corner of the hotel which sold them was locked and no-one could find the keys.

Outside, a group of five pedlars sat in a line, offering brass daggers with turquoise scabbards and other examples of the art of the fierce Tuareg warriors who, throughout the history of Timbuctoo, would periodically sweep in from the desert and take over the town. Now even they have been defeated by the sands. The soil which once supported the wiry cram-cram grass on which their camels fed has disappeared under a blanket of white dust. Occasionally it is possible to glimpse beneath the several inches of sand the baked clay surface of what was once a fertile loam. But that is rare. The only place where

anything grows now is in the gardens which have been dug, like massive cones 30 feet deep and 100 yards across, around the settlement's few dozen boreholes.

All around Timbuctoo the huge dunes of sand are creeping onwards, thousands of tons at the rate of 20 miles a year. The fine white powder falls like a curse from the heavens; often there is so much of it in the air that the sun is blotted out for days on end. There is an apocalyptic quality to living with the earth above your head for so long.

Above At this season the well should be full. But the women are pulling only muddy water from 60 metres down.
Right top Wild nuts and berries, all there is to eat at Bogoya.
Right below Almost all the able-bodied men in the village have gone to find work in the Ivory Coast. This weaver is one of the few to remain. Bogoya, Burkina Faso.

Above Galvanizing peasants to volunteer for construction projects, near Ouahigouya, Burkina Faso. *Right* Babies on their backs, stones in their hands: mothers at work on the dam. *Overleaf* Bored with official explanations, Geldof stalks off to talk to the journalists.

On the way back to the airport the Band Aid landrovers stopped, and Geldof gazed out over the dunes which stretched for more than 1000 miles beyond the horizon.

To the north of Timbuctoo, the nomads say, there once lay a town called Erewan. Its name bears a remarkable similarity to the place created by Samuel Butler in his 19th-century satire *Erehwon* (readers were supposed to spell it backwards to grasp the implications). Few people go to Erewan these days, for it is a nowhere town too. It will not be long before a string of other towns along the margins of the Sahara join it beneath the sands of time.

OUAGADOUGOU

The Prince Charles syndrome

The BA 125 soared through the dust that shrouds Mali and headed east. Beneath us the land stretched to the horizon, parched, brown and featureless. Back in our mobile home we sank contentedly into the plush upholstery and the delights of Western technology. Tim Rex slotted the other film, *Raiders of the Lost Ark*, into the video machine; Cyril served drinks with ice from the fridge; Geldof began reading Trivial Pursuit cards to himself, which is, perhaps, why he is so good at it; and Jenden played with the executive telephone fixed to the cabin wall next to his seat. "Sell Mali," he barked into the phone. "Buy Hawaii. Take an option on Sudan, futures on Gabon." Then he called his wife. The pilots patched the call through from the plane, which was at 40,000 feet over Central Africa, via a network of satellites and relay stations. Within a few seconds the phone was ringing in Jenden's home in Stoke Newington, London. His wife answered. Like many technological miracles, it only half worked. "Hello, it's Kevin, over," said Jenden, and lifted the button on the receiver so his wife could speak. "Hello, hello, it's Kevin, over." "Yes, I'm flying over Mali, over." "What, over." "Over Mali, M-A-L-I, over." "What, over." "I can't hear you, over." "I said I can't hear you, over." Several of us made horrendously expensive collect calls to our home numbers. One or two words broke through, muffled by crackle and hiss.

Geldof leafed through the files on Burkina Faso, the next country on the itinerary. Our collective knowledge about Burkina was slim and mostly wrong. Someone had heard that it had recently changed its name from Upper Volta to

Burkina Faso because the President, Thomas Sankara, was sick of being the last to speak at African conferences where countries are called in alphabetical order. "Sounds like crap," said Geldof. He had heard that Sankara, who took over in a military coup, played the electric guitar and liked Bob Marley. Geldof has a poor opinion of all politicians, regardless of colour or ideology. It extends to African leaders. "I've never heard of an African leader I would want to give the time of day to," said Geldof. "My rule is, be polite to every lance corporal you meet because

likely as not he'll be the president when you go back." Jenden had invented a question for the African version of Trivial Pursuit: "Name three people who have not been president of Nigeria."

Geldof's copy of *Africa Confidential* painted a stark picture of life in Burkina. Sankara had narrowly missed death on a visit to the neighbouring Ivory Coast when a bomb exploded in the bathroom of his hotel suite, luckily just before his arrival. Relations had "cooled further", said *Africa Confidential*, when a leading Burkinan businessman was assassinated

on a visit to the Ivory Coast. Relations with Libya had also cooled after Colonel Gadaffi demanded payment for arms he had supplied. Sankara faced opposition at home. The extreme left wing was disaffected and the professionals and bourgeoisie were rebelling against swingeing austerity cuts. There had been unrest in the capital Ouagadougou. The economy continued to deteriorate. The budgetary deficit had grown. Thirty per cent of the gross national product went to service debts.

"Sankara is in deep shit," said Geldof. "On the whole I would say that is a fair

assessment of the situation pertaining in Burkina Faso," a Western diplomat in the capital was later to tell us.

The country also served as a model of how international aid had failed to work. Burkina was reputed to have been the recipient of more aid per capita and host to more aid organizations than any other country. Despite this, the drought had taken a heavy toll, and little Burkina not only had had to look after its own starving people but also had been inundated with famine refugees from Mali and Niger. Sankara's revolutionary Government seemed to have only a precarious grip on power, but, according to the aid reports, the young President had stamped down on the sort of corruption and inefficiency that plagued Mali, for example. Cabinet ministers had been sent out to work in the fields. Officials were on trial in Ouagadougou for corruption, including customs frauds and the misuse of aid funds. And the people had been spurred by revolutionary zeal into a concerted attack on famine.

All in all Sankara seemed to be Geldof's kind of military dictator. He was looking forward to meeting him.

The jet taxied into Ouagadougou airport and Geldof peered through the window. "Christ almighty!" he shouted. "Cyril, tell the pilots to take off. I don't believe it." Stretched along the tarmac was a welcoming committee of a size that might impress even the Queen. Geldof was appalled. The press corps was delighted, and Bill Nicol, the BBC cameraman, shoved Geldof through the door and down the steps. The Government of Burkina greeted him with revolutionary fervour. A long line of small boys wearing what looked like Cubs uniforms began chanting "Welcome, welcome, Bob Geldof". They were called the Little Singers of the Raised Fist. They were joined in the chanting by a female singing group, the Doves of the Revolution, and dozens of Burkinan dignitaries. Geldof moved down the line shaking hands. The Government had another revolutionary treat in store at the airport terminal, where half a dozen scantily clad Burkinan maidens began moving their hips provocatively to frenzied drum music.

A diplomat in the reception committee said that by the hospitable standards of Burkina this was rock-bottom protocol and it meant they were hardly pleased to see Geldof at all. For important guests the tarmac was jammed with chanting and dancing figures and raised fists. The welcome could go on for hours. "He has got off lightly," he said.

"We asked for as little protocol as possible," said the Red Cross man, pleading for understanding.

"Well, you didn't ask loud enough," said Geldof as he extricated himself from the shimmying women. With a scowl he got into the official car.

It was the first attack of what Geldof calls the Prince Charles Syndrome, or PCS

for short. This is not a jibe at Prince Charles, and in fact Geldof has discussed the phenomenon with him at Kensington Palace. Charles has to play the protocol game, and privately bemoans the fact that he can rarely, if ever, talk unofficially and candidly to ordinary people. Geldof wants to be seen and treated as a serious person, which he is, not as a celebrity. He wanted to meet real people and the famine experts and to cut protocol and those empty, formal government meetings down to a bare minimum. Geldof, however, is a star. He is perhaps better known in Africa than

Above **Local boys bemused by the Geldof entourage.** *Right* **Geldof plants a tree in the Grove of the Fourth of August, date of the Burkina Faso revolution.**

FACTORS IN THE FAMINE
THE DEATH OF AN ANCIENT TRADITION

The people who have been worst hit by the present drought and famine are the nomads who depend entirely on their livestock for a living. In many parts of the Sahel these people have lost 85 per cent of their animals. Many have lost them all.

There is a tendency in the West to regard nomads as the most feckless and primitive of African groups. It dates, as environmentalist Lloyd Timberlake points out, from the Victorian theory that pastoralism is a stage of human development more "modern" than hunting but less advanced than settled farming and the industrialization which can only be built on an agricultural surplus. But, like so many of the theories applied in recent years to Africa, it is subconsciously based on the false notion that, with the appropriate technology, great areas of the continent could be turned into farmland like that in the temperate climatic zones of Europe and the USA.

NOMADIC PAST

The reality is somewhat different. The latest studies show that in Mali nomadic pastoralism is the most effective way of using more than 80 per cent of the country's total land surface. The figure is similar for most of the countries in the Sahelian belt.

What nomads do by shifting their animals around the scant grazing of the dry grasslands is, in effect, to gather and store the meagre resources of large areas in a concentrated and mobile form—their cattle, goats, sheep and camels. Over the generations these herders have developed finely tuned techniques for getting their herds and flocks quickly to the pockets of new grass created by localized showers, which is twice as digestible as dry grass. Far from being primitive, it is highly skilled, and is probably the only possible productive use of these desiccated rangelands.

But the position of nomads in African society, as elsewhere in the world, has always been a difficult one.

Often treated as pariahs by settled peoples, as are the gypsies of Europe, they engage in trades or occupations which are considered ignoble, such as metal work, leather tanning or pottery; they often bear reputations as poisoners and sorcerers. The rulers of the countries in which they wander are almost invariably drawn from the tribes of settled farmers rather than from the nomads, despite the fact that in a country like Niger 75 per cent of the population is from the great Tuareg and Fulani nomadic tribes. Sympathy for the herders is scant; to a government nomads are armed, unruly, uncontrolled and untaxed people who possess large quantities of what could be good beef for export. They could be worse than that: in Niger President Kountche suspects that many of the Tuareg tribesmen are in league with Libya in plots against his regime.

PITCHED BATTLES

In times of crisis, discrimination against the nomads is heightened. In Mali, for example, aid workers report that it is difficult for nomads to receive food aid because it is distributed only to people who are at present in the areas where they were first registered. In Niger there are no land rights over common pasture, only over cultivated land. Hence farmers can move unchecked into territory north of the line where less than 300mm of rain falls every year. This is traditionally seasonal pastureland and is unsuitable for ploughing without running the risk of turning it to desert. But when nomads move south to look for alternative pastures, their arrival is often deeply resented by local farmers. In the Intakashin area of Niger there have been pitched battles with bows and arrows and spears as a result of this friction.

Now that their animals are dead, many nomads are left stranded, refugees in unwelcoming shanty towns, with no sense of purpose. Livestock to them was more than a source of food. It was a form of

money, of investment, and a measure of social standing. Without animals the people are demoralized.

CHILDREN SOLD

The traditional mechanism for repairing this social breakdown has fallen apart. In the past when a Fulani nomad was in need a richer herder would lend him a cow which he would keep for the time it took to have three calves and then return to its owner. The problem is that in 1985 there are not enough animals left to operate the old system. The Kabbashi nomads in northern Kordofan in Sudan, for example, lost 95 per cent of their camels. Elsewhere in the Sahel, 85 per cent losses were commonplace. After the 1968–73 drought an aid programme was set up based on this traditional system: by stepping in before the people became destitute it allowed them to continue their normal way of life. But now things have gone too far. In Niger they are comparing 1985 to the famine of 1903, which had two names: The Year of the Crushed Calabash, because people powdered their water-gourds and ate them, and The Year of the Sold Children, because some families were reduced to selling their offspring in the hope that as slaves they would have a better chance of survival.

So the nomads have been forced to look for alternative ways of regeneration. Some, who were forced early in the drought to sell their cattle to rich tradesmen, have since hired them back from the buyers. It is an insidious form of debt-trap from which the nomads can never extricate themselves. Others have made the effort to invest their energies in settled agriculture in Mali, Niger and Chad, but with mixed results. And aid workers feel they may be creating even worse problems for the long-term. "By putting them all in one place you make extra difficulties with sanitation, health and education," said one American relief worker. "The fear is that, if then the crops fail, we will have created a new disaster."

Prince Charles. He was travelling with a television team. Naturally Burkina Faso was going to milk the trip for all the international publicity it was worth.

The chanting of the Little Singers of the Raised Fist still ringing in his ears, Geldof drove to the Hôtel Indépendance in a convoy of small black cars. The official fleet of Mercedes had recently been sold off by the President as an austerity measure. Although, as we would see next day, the Burkinan countryside is desperately poor, the city of Ouagadougou, built in the French-colonial style with wide boulevards, trees and large official buildings, looks fairly prosperous. There are traffic jams of mopeds, which roar in

their thousands down the streets. Revolutionary slogans promoting the People's Struggle of President Sankara festoon the former presidential offices, which have been renamed the People's Palace.

At the Hôtel Indépendance Geldof scrutinized the schedule. "That's out," he said. "I'm not meeting another Minister of Sport and Culture." He also baulked at a meeting with the Minister of Families and National Solidarity. The protocol officials pleaded and cajoled. As usual, Geldof relented, and later that day he found himself at the Ministry.

"Who's the boiler over there," said Geldof, pointing at a tall, striking lady with long legs. The boiler (Geldof's affec-

Right **Lords of the desert. Tuareg tribesmen at Agadez, Niger.** *Overleaf* **A Fulani woman, one of the feminists of the desert.**

tionate term for women) happened to be Josephine Ouedraogo, the Minister of Families and National Solidarity. She is a member of the new wave of Burkinan politicians in Sankara's cabinet, young and radical, part of the pro-Chinese faction, the Union des Luttes Communistes. Ouedraogo, who seemed cooler to Geldof's charms than he to hers, bleakly outlined the problems: despite good rains which had broken the long drought and improved prospects for a crop, the emer-

gency still affected 2.5 million of the seven million population and there were 200,000 people displaced by the drought. The Government was not dealing with this in the classic way, by asking for more aid, she said, deftly omitting to mention the fact that about 50 per cent of Burkina's budget is derived from what the aid jargon calls "donor sources". The Government was trying to build a programme of national self-reliance, she said. The population must participate at all levels.

"Fine, fine," said Geldof, anxious to be off to get to grips with the problems of famine.

But before he could do that, Burkina had another urgent problem and needed Geldof's advice. Reluctantly he had agreed to see the Minister of Sport and Culture and for once he was kept waiting—in a small, stifling office where he promptly fell asleep. The Minister, a severe young man with steel-rimmed spectacles, woke him up half an hour later. The Minister, who had heard about the stunning success of the Live Aid concert, wanted Geldof's advice on arranging an international festival of music in the Burkinan capital the next spring. Geldof was incredulous. "What, you mean live from Ouagadougou?"

That is exactly what the Minister meant. "I thought of getting all our traditional singers and dancers to perform and then inviting international stars, like you."

"Yes, well, I'm very tied up this spring as a matter of fact," said Geldof. "But I will tell you what to do."

"Thank you," said the Minister.

"Don't put on the ethnic dancers and singers, it will turn people off."

"Turn them off?" said the Minister.

"Yeah. Boring. You want to scrap the ethnic crap and get in some of the American superstars like Michael Jackson and Lionel Ritchie."

The Minister's interest was aroused. He cleaned his glasses.

"Look, I'll tell you how to do it. It isn't very revolutionary but it works and you'll make money. First you ring up the TV companies. You've got to have TV, that's where the money is. You tell them that you've got Michael Jackson playing and do they want live satellite feed. That

might be tricky, so you could tape it and flog them the tape. Then you ring up Jackson's agent and you tell him the television companies are taking a feed live from Ouagadougou. Does he want to come? Of course he wants to come. Then

46

you ring up the other rock stars and say, 'We've got everyone else.' Then they'll come. You make a lot of money, they make a lot of money. Got it? Another thing. You need a good sound system and the best one is British, so get your embassy to fix it.''

The Minister's secretary made notes. "Thank you, Mr Geldof," said the Minister. "We look forward to 'Live from Ouagadougou'.''

"Yeah, great,'' said Geldof. "I'll watch it on the TV.''

Geldof will remember his first evening in Ouagadougou for a very long time. During the rest of the trip it was to haunt him. He had been invited as the guest of honour to a concert in the officers' mess in Ouagadougou. It was very hot. Geldof sat sweating and swiping at giant mosquitoes in the centre of a row of chairs facing the stage while the host, a member of the Government Information Ministry and Burkina's answer to Bruce Forsyth, shouted revolutionary slogans over the crackling loud-speaker system. Hundreds of Burkinans had turned up for the show and so had a large part of the insect population of Africa. Millions of mosquitoes, moths and beetles, attracted by the arc lights, swarmed to the officers' mess.

Then, through the haze of insects, Geldof saw the Little Singers of the Raised Fist take the stand. They played a strange version of Western pop music interspersed with strident revolutionary songs. They were joined by the Doves of the Revolution, the Namande troupe, the Nankana troupe, the troupe of Naba Yadega. The girls who had caught Geldof at the airport that morning danced out of

the gloom, weaving and shimmying. They prostrated themselves at Geldof's feet. He smiled nervously. They presented him with a skin drum. He banged it tentatively with the little stick provided. There was a roll of drums from the Little Raised Fists, and the host walked over and invited Geldof to sing a song. He refused. The host took his arm and like a Redcoat at Butlins heaved him to his feet. Geldof shambled over to the stage. The band struck up what they took to be a rock and roll number. Geldof shook a castanet limply for a few seconds then dashed back

to his chair. He sank down, tapping his skin drum. The concert went on for three hours.

In the bar of the Hôtel Indépendance that night Geldof exploded. "That's it. No more. That's the sodding PCS. I was in a no-win situation. If I refuse to go up on the stage I'm being rude. If I sing I look like a dick. How can I sing along with those little Raised Fist bleeders? The band was crap. Christ that was awful. Three hours being bitten to death and listening to that. Christ. That's it. Hey Morris," he said to the BBC reporter. "Did you film that? I

Their animals dead, Tuareg nomads have turned to agriculture. Their first crop is a failure. Agadez, Niger.
Overleaf **For 2000 years his ancestors roamed the desert. A nomadic herdsman whose animals have died, facing a life of dependency at a settlement run by the Red Cross, Agadez, Niger.**

bet you did, you bastard. That will be all over the television tomorrow night."

"I might have got just a few seconds of it, Bob," said Morris. They appeared, those few seconds, all over the television screens in Britain the next night.

The Red Cross officials organizing the Band Aid tour went into the telex room of the Indépendance and started firing off dispatches to Chad, Sudan and Ethiopia, cutting all protocol out of the schedules. Any even remote hint of Prince Charles Syndrome had to be expurgated.

Our brief introduction to President Sankara's revolutionary ideology left a confused impression. It was an odd mixture, with the pro-Chinese Josephine Ouedraogo, pro-Albanians from the Partie Communiste Révolutionnaire Voltaique, the pro-Soviet Ligue Patriotique pour le Développement, and revolutionary slogans with clear Cuban antecedents. It was not truly Marxist, and relations with the Soviet Union were chilly. It was anti-colonial and anti-Western, although

Western aid workers said that the people were polite and friendly and did not bear the resentment of more fervent regimes. Sankara had made a bold effort to fight the famine. He had organized the army to help in transportation and relief. He had cut wages by half. "I think that with Sankara in Burkina Faso they could crack the famine," said Geldof. "The Government is pragmatic. It is not tied into an ideology. It has a centralized system and it is not asking for food aid, it is not going with a begging bowl to the industrialized world." On the other hand, Sankara ran a tight and, many believed, brutal regime. He had imprisoned teachers and civil servants who went on strike, and banned unions. There were too many allegations of torture to ignore. Burkina had the trappings of a potentially vicious dictatorship.

Sankara had invited Geldof to a private audience, and Geldof, considerately, had asked if he could bring the hacks along. Sankara agreed. We drove to the palace at

night in a convoy of cars with government officials and armed guards. It was an eerie place. The roads around the palace were deserted and blocked by army patrols. We were stopped several times. "It is very dangerous here," said our driver, a member of the Red Cross. "The guards are nervous." We had a soldier in the back seat. When he went to the main checkpoint the guard aimed his automatic rifle at him. Our soldier walked with his hands up, rifle in the air. The guard frisked him and looked at his papers. There is not a lot of trust in the Burkinan army.

We waited in a palace anteroom where young men in army fatigues, with automatic rifles and dark glasses, lolled on Louis XV chairs and settees. They were the President's praetorian guard or innermost circle of defence. We were then taken down a corridor to where a soldier sat in the corner, like a corporal on duty outside the President's office. It was President

Above Waiting at the oasis. *Right* Geldof filming the scene at the oasis. The few surviving animals are healthy because there is now less competition for grazing and water. Agadez, Niger.

Sankara. He explained he did not use his office and preferred to sit in the corridor to set a revolutionary example to his people. As an economy measure, he did not use air conditioning. The corridor was cramped and hot. Mosquitoes swarmed.

Geldof asked if it were true, as the human rights organization Amnesty International had claimed, that he tortured his political opponents.

"Not true at all," said the President with a fixed smile. "In fact I have had a letter of apology from Amnesty about that report. We did have some little people who were plotting against us and our reaction was violent. We killed them. That would have been done in any country to people guilty of treason. But now there are more coups and we will not execute

them. We will call the press to watch the trials by the people's tribunals."

"Do the people in the tribunals have any legal training?" asked Geldof.

"No, but sometimes justice is more important than law."

"That is what Robespierre said. People are open to jealousies, malice and envy. You have to have a legal framework."

"We will have trials. Anyway, some of those people, many of them, will be released next week, or the week after. I will organize it."

"But that's just your personal whim. That's not justice."

Sankara ignored the point and carried on with his main theme.

"Last year we found people who intended to assassinate the leadership. In foreign countries there are regimes who don't like us because of our struggle against the bourgeoisie. They insult us. They organize against us. And they have the help of businessmen and the big traditional chiefs."

"In short," Sankara said, "running a small African independent country is like being a rebellious musician on a big record label. Your opponents look for the worst image. I have executed people who plotted a coup against me. But I do not use torture. These are stories put about by my enemies in the bourgeoisie because I am a man of the people and I play the guitar. The guitar for me is a means to be acceptable to the people but my enemies say it proves I am a druggie and a bad man." Geldof nodded.

With large circular motions of his arms, Sankara continued to outline his philosophy: "In Burkina 97 per cent of the people live off the land. Yet of 57 billion francs in the national budget 15 billion are spent in the capital on hotels, electricity, carpets and other things the people do not have. It is for the elite, the people I went to school with. Yet they are three per cent of the population. Is this fair?

"I say no. So I have introduced austerity measures. I make diplomats sleep on the floor in their offices instead of using hotel rooms. I make them eat sandwiches instead of expensive lunches. I make them drive in small cars. The city is no longer happy. I do not allow the import of French cheese, wines and perfumes. I diminish their wages. They are not happy. I myself am no longer happy because I too am a little bourgeois like them."

"Why is that?" asked Geldof.

"Well, there are things I cannot do," said Sankara. "When I was a little boy I saw presidents in big cars and I can't even have that pleasure because I got rid of all the Mercedes. I can't even have the air conditioning on. When I went to the Organization of African Unity conference in Addis Ababa I had to hitchhike back to Burkina. I asked many presidents for a lift home and most of them said no."

Sankara, a little like Geldof, prefers broad themes to detail. He said he had refused American and Soviet aid because the superpowers attached conditions to it. When we pressed him for details of these conditions, he grew uneasy, then hostile. We asked for facts and figures. Men in dark glasses with large bulges under their shirts stepped between us.

"No more questions. No more questions," they announced. From behind, officials pulled us firmly away. Our

Above **The préfet of Agadez presents a Tuareg camel saddle to Geldof, face blue from the dye of his local headscarf.** *Right top* **Barber's shop, Agadez, Niger.** *Below* **At Niamey, capital of Niger.**

audience was over. Geldof stayed on for a few minutes and Sankara asked him if he would like to start a group. Sankara claims to play a mean electric guitar, Geldof could sing and Sankara's friend Flight Lieutenant Jerry Rawlings, the President of Ghana, could play the drums. "I'm a bit busy at the moment," said Geldof. "But you could try the former King of Thailand. He plays the saxophone."

As a parting gesture of friendship Geldof gave Sankara a Live Aid T-shirt and a tape of Bob Marley. It was not such a generous gesture, as Geldof had borrowed the Marley tape from someone in the press corps. Sankara was delighted. "Bob, that's another thing I can't do. I have banned the import of music tape as part of my austerity measures. If you could send me some by post I would be very grateful."

If Geldof does so he might include in the package a copy of the human rights report which Amnesty International in London is quite emphatic it has not withdrawn. It tells a horrifying and well-substantiated story of torture by electric shock and sexual abuse. The victims include civil servants, a teacher, a policeman and a former paratrooper who was tortured to death by revolutionaries who cut him open and burned his insides with a blowtorch. Amnesty is still awaiting a reply from the smiling President on that one.

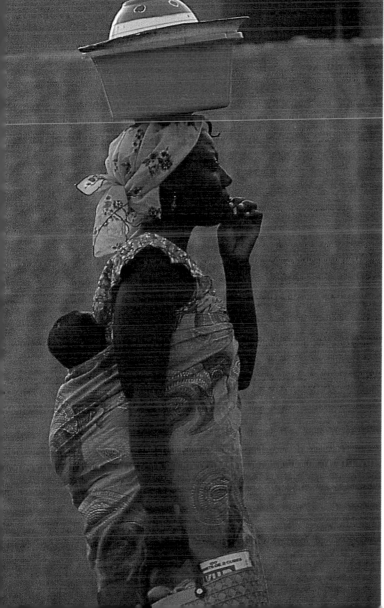

FACTORS IN THE FAMINE
SPENDING ON GUNS NOT GRAIN

In the 20th century, famine can no longer be regarded as a natural phenomenon: it is the mismanagement of drought, and it is no coincidence that the five African countries which have suffered most from famine over the past 12 months—Ethiopia, Sudan, Chad, Angola and Mozambique—also happen to be the five African countries engaged in the most bitter civil wars.

The two most essential prerequisites for successful development are peace and political stability. Yet in 1984, the year of the great famine, the cost of importing arms into Africa exceeded, for the first time ever, the cost of importing food.

ARMS BUDGET

Ethiopia, the country whose starving millions aroused the conscience of the world, in 1984 spent an estimated 47 per cent of its total annual income on arms. In addition to that it continues to build up a debt to the Soviet Union, now said to exceed $2000 million, in prosecution of wars against the Eritreans who have been fighting for independence in the north for 24 years and against smaller rebel groups in Tigre and Wollo. These areas have been neglected by successive Ethiopian governments under the Emperor Haile Selassie and the Marxist military regime which overthrew him in 1974, both dominated by the ruling minority Amhara peoples. Aid has taken second place, quite literally, to armaments. Even at the height of the famine, despite government promises that certain berths in the port of Assab would be reserved for off-loading food aid, ships with grain were forced to wait at anchor while Soviet cargo ships carrying artillery, tanks, ammunition and bombs were unloaded in the reserved berths.

By contrast, in Niger in 1985 one of the major factors which softened the blow of the famine was that its army was free to throw its full resources into the distribution of food aid. The Ethiopian army, the largest in black Africa, was busy with other activities.

CIVIL WARS

The civil wars in Africa do not simply divert money from relief and development work; they can also directly harm the food-growing potential of the land. In Sudan, where the Muslim-dominated Government has been fighting an off-and-on war with the black Christians in the south for more than 20 years, both rebels and tribes armed by the Government have a history of laying waste the land in great military surges of looting and pillage. In Ethiopia fleeing farmers report that the army pursues a "scorched earth" policy of deliberately destroying the homes, crops, livestock and fields of peasants it suspects may be rebel sympathizers. In Chad, too, farmers are driven from their land by the civil war and into exile to the camps in the west of Sudan.

The United Nations estimates that there are now ten million refugees in Africa—all of them an added burden on their host nation, all of them having abandoned a more useful and productive way of life in the process.

Civil war also hampers the work of foreign relief agencies. In Ethiopia, German and British aid workers in Lalibela and Korem have been kidnapped by rebels, and a group of American charity workers narrowly escaped the same fate in Barentu in 1985. On the other side of the same war, doctors from Oxfam behind the rebel lines were bombarded by Soviet-built MiGs from the Ethiopian airforce. In the summer of 1985, in the south of Sudan, Voluntary Service Overseas (VSO) pulled all its workers out of the southern capital of Juba, after more than a decade of development work in the area, because of the deteriorating security situation. The Dutch had already removed a consultant from a rice project and the British and Italians had withdrawn staff from tea plantations. When the rebels threatened to shoot down all aircraft, even aid planes, the UN itself called its staff out of Wau and Rumbeck. In Chad, throughout the famine, it proved impossible for relief workers to get food to the far north of the country, where the forces of the rebels and the occupying Libyan army run a heavily restrictive system of pass laws to prevent free movement.

But undoubtedly the greatest problem caused by war is that it puts a stop to development that could dramatically curtail the major problems of the entire famine belt.

WASTED POTENTIAL

The soils of Chad are so fertile that—given a degree of mechanization, better strains of seeds, fertilizers, insecticides, and sensible soil and water conservation measures—the country could grow enough to feed the entire Sahelian region and still have a grain surplus to export. But there is small hope of that while the Chadian Government is fighting two separate civil wars and has a hostile Libya illegally occupying almost one third of its country.

The south of Sudan offers even greater opportunity. The area is rich in fertile soils, timber, minerals like gold, and has some of the best potential in the continent for wildlife tourism—it is one of the few places in Africa where the white rhino survives. The region is bisected by the longest river in the world, where the possibilities for hydroelectric power and clean water schemes are considerable. Beneath the ground is what is thought to be the biggest oil reserve in Africa. Chevron, which invested $90 million in developing the field until the war made them close down the operation, estimates a possible output of 50,000 barrels a day, producing an income of $250 million a year.

Yet today in the main hospital in Juba there is no water and no power. And those who require an injection are expected to bring their own needle and syringe.

BURKINA

A revolutionary solution

Everywhere that Geldof went he was followed by a silent young man wearing dark glasses.

"Who's that bloke," he asked the lady from the Ministry of Protocol.

"He is your bodyguard," she said.

"I don't need a bodyguard," said Geldof. But the man with dark glasses would not be moved. He stayed with Geldof, a few feet away at most, day and night, his hand nonchalantly inside his jacket, resting on the bulge beneath his arm. That first night Geldof had tried to take pity on him. He bought him dinner and a drink, rather than have him sit silently at the next table. Afterwards he said, through an interpreter, "You can shove off now. I'm fine, honest. Go home and get a good night's sleep."

"I never sleep," said the man in the dark glasses.

To prove the point he stood at night outside Geldof's door or lurked just around the corner in the corridor. When Bill Nicol went by arrangement to wake

Right top N'Djamena, three years after the fighting. *Right below* On the Avenue Charles de Gaulle, N'Djamena's main street. *Overleaf* Petrol by the bottle: a filling station, N'Djamena, Chad.

Geldof at 6 am the next morning, the man with the dark glasses dashed around the corner and jammed the TV cameraman up against the wall.

Geldof heard the commotion and came to the door. Despite his hatred of all the pomp and ceremony he seemed quite to enjoy having his own bodyguard. "It's OK," he said, with a regal wave of the hand. "You can let him go."

It was an early start, for the real

problems in Burkina Faso were to be found in the four northern provinces. They were not a huge distance away but there was no suitable landing strip for the BA 125. There was, truth to tell, no landing strip for even the smallest aircraft. Indeed, once at the edge of the famine-hit area there are no roads to speak of, which is why food distribution is so difficult.

We travelled in a convoy of landrovers through a city which, even at that early hour, had been about its business for some time, and took the road to Yatenga, the most accessible of the northern provinces. In the suburbs of Ouagadougou we passed large areas that looked like bomb sites, whole districts in which all the buildings had been totally flattened. Further out many of the houses at the side of the road were marked with a large white cross.

"These will be pulled down too," said a government official from the Protocol Department.

"It's a slum clearance programme, then, is it?" asked Geldof.

"In a way. President Sankara has looked at satellite pictures of Ouagadougou and compared them with the city plans of 1973. Every house which has been built since then without planning permission . . ."

". . . which seems to be most of them," interjected Geldof, peering out of the landrover window.

". . . is marked with a white cross and then pulled down."

"That'll teach the bastards to build their hovels without planning permission," Geldof said to no-one in particular. "You can't accuse old Sankara of being indecisive," he added with a grin for the benefit of his journalistic entourage.

Only a few miles out of the city the convoy turned off the tarmac road and down a bumpy track to the Grove of the Fourth of August, named after the date of the 1984 coup which brought Captain Sankara to power.

"You are to plant a tree in the revolutionary grove," the person from Protocol informed Geldof as the landrover jerked to a sudden halt.

"Oh f . . .," said Geldof. "Why didn't you get Prince Charles to come and do it. This is not what I came here to do."

"Prince who?" said the person from Protocol.

"OK. Never mind. Where's the f . . . ing tree?"

The tree in question had, in fact, been left behind on the Ouagadougou road along with the forester who was carrying it. A landrover roared off in a cloud of orange dust in search. Ten minutes later it returned bearing a diminutive forester who wore an apologetic grin. The man got out and produced a small sapling about two feet in height. With a single-bladed pick he dug a small hole, then with a machete neatly trimmed the black plastic wrapping from the roots, placed the plant in the hole and pushed the surrounding soil swiftly into place.

"Hang on. Who's supposed to be plant-

ing this f . . . ing tree," asked Geldof as the forester took a battered old aluminium watering can to soak the sapling.

"This is just a demonstration of the technique," said the person from Protocol, who made a living out of such things. "Your tree is over there."

"Christ, I'm here to see a f . . . ing famine not take lessons in f . . . ing forestry."

Geldof, with a clumsiness surprising in a son of the Celtic turf, bullied the ground into a hole with his pick and then repeated the planting routine.

"I declare this tree well and truly planted," he said, squashing the soil around the little acacia into place with his familiar piratical boot. "Can we go now?"

"Now there is Mr Jenden's tree."

"Oh f . . . ing hell."

Jenden seized the pick and swung it

wildly. The soil flew in all directions.

"Watch it!" shouted Geldof.

"Well, I'm supposed to be an architect not a bloody manual labourer," said Jenden, and to prove the point swung the machete with such poor aim that he chopped the roots off his sapling.

"You understand about roots, do you, Kev?"

"Well, I haven't read the book but I saw the film," quipped Jenden, reaching for the watering can.

"OK," said Geldof. "Can we . . ."

"Now there is the tree for *The Times*."

"Oh f . . . me," said Geldof, turning his back in resignation.

After Vallely's demonstration of his considerable agricultural skills, which included inadvertently planting his biro, there came the BBC tree. And after the BBC tree there came the speeches.

Bringing in food aid across the Chari River, from Cameroon into Chad. Band Aid will build a bridge here.

"You are Bob Geldof."

"I am Bob Geldof," repeated the subject.

"You have travelled in many lands."

"I have travelled in many lands."

Eventually it came to an end. "Now we can go," said the person from Protocol.

"Are you sure there isn't a little hoeing you'd like us to do while we're here?" said Geldof as he was bundled into his vehicle.

The next stop was two hours later at a massive reservoir created by one of the 200 dams the country has built in the recent past. "Where we have built the dams there will be no more famine," said a government official. This one was a dam from early in the programme and not

considered a total success — too big, too shallow and not serving enough people.

"Can you tell me, on a one-to-one basis, how the decision making process is arrived at . . ." began Jenden.

"Yeah, who decides where to put them?" interrupted Geldof with his gift for summary.

The government officials held forth about the dam while behind their backs aid workers complained about the choice of project.

"I don't know why they've brought you here. I expect it's because it's big and impressive-looking," said one United Nations official. "But in fact it's a pretty useless dam. The water evaporates too easily. But the smaller, more recent ones they've built are really excellent. You wouldn't think it from this example but this Government is one of the few in Africa

to have learned the lesson that big is not necessarily beautiful and that the future lies in small-scale projects motivated by local initiative."

Geldof was to see such a project later in the day. But before it there was a depressing prelude.

"I want to see an ordinary village," he announced suddenly, "one that is not on the official itinerary." The Band Aid convoy took a detour along a dusty road where rain had obviously not fallen for weeks. The track ended at the little village of Bogoya.

The crop was five feet high in the fields around the cluster of mud buildings, yet amidst the tall plants cattle roamed. The thin-ribbed beasts trampled the millet beneath their feet and chewed among the crumpled stems. By the side of the road and at the doors of their dwellings dispirited peasants sat and watched, making no attempt to shoo the beasts away.

"The rains were good but two and a half million people are still affected by famine": these were the bald statistics Geldof had been given in the capital. Here was the reality.

The early prospects for the 1985 harvest had been good. After a year of drought, which the old men who could remember it compared with the terrible year of 1920, the rains had come. They were ample in July and August in Burkina Faso, and the crops grew well. But in September the farmers searched the skies in vain for rain-bearing clouds. Slowly the realization dawned that the vital rains were not to come. The plants had been fully pollinated and had formed seeds. But the tiny black kernels, dry and hard as little grains of sand, had not swollen to ripeness. The entire crop was useless, fit only for fodder for the few cattle which survived the drought. The story, the UN officials said, was the same in a thousand villages throughout the four northern provinces.

"Can we speak to the headman?" asked Geldof. He and Jenden were introduced to him, an old man sitting on a log by the entrance to the village—a labyrinth of mud walls connecting houses, granaries, kitchens, refuse areas, like a miniature version of a medieval European city.

"The cattle eat our crop. There is nothing for us. Our young men have all left and gone to another country," said the village elder.

"Most go to the Ivory Coast," said one experienced aid worker, beginning a running commentary. "It is the richest country in the region. They hope to make their fortunes there—along with the other two million newcomers who have arrived there in the past year."

"Our well has only mud. It is 60 metres deep and at this time of year should have water. But it has none," said the old man. He wore a queer pointed hat which, if he had ever smiled, would have made him look like a pixie. But he did not smile, not once. "We have no food."

61

"This may sound callous, but the old man has had many white men visit him in the past. He has learned to say the things they want to hear," said the aid worker. "In fact there is a little food in the cereal bank which stores this village's grain. Not much, but enough to last until January."

"And after that?"

The aid worker shrugged. "It is a long time between January and October, which is when the harvest is gathered in."

"May we have a look around inside?" asked Geldof.

"I'm sorry that I can't invite you into my house," said the headman. "In my country you can't invite a guest to enter unless you have something to offer him. I have nothing."

"That's OK. Thanks anyway," said Geldof, and shaking the old man's hand he added, "We'll just have a look around the village." He walked off into the narrow entrance, unslinging the inevitable video camera from his shoulder.

The aid workers were outraged.

"He has just walked all over local etiquette," said one. "He has just asked if he can go in. The headman said no. Then he walks in anyway."

But the headman had been talking of his house, someone protested.

"The house and the village are the same thing here. Get him out of there with that bloody camera. This is dreadful. This is just tourism."

But Geldof was not to be removed. He toured the village silently, tracking and backtracking along the maze of paths which led from empty granaries to bare houses. In one he found an old man lying, not sleeping but resting, on a rush mat

Top **Spur of the moment fishing in the Chari River.** *Above* **Scraping flour from the bottom of the transport boat.** *Right* **Boys scavenge for flour as the boat is unloaded.** *Overleaf* **Mother and child at the main hospital, N'Djamena, Chad.**

inside the doorway of his home. He opened his eyes at Geldof's approach and painfully raised himself to a sitting position. He was as thin as a Belsen victim, a skeleton covered in wrinkled black skin. His eyes stared unblinking at the strange apparition. Slowly he raised his empty hand to his mouth in a ghastly mime of someone eating from a bowl of food. Geldof stood and looked. The mime continued; this bowl was obviously full of the invisible substance. Geldof watched. The man's hand moved mechanically; his eyes never left the white man's. Then Geldof's nerve broke. He turned his head and walked slowly away.

Outside the village one of the aid workers was complaining. "He shouldn't have gone in. He should have been stopped."

Geldof walked slowly past.

"There's an old man dying in there," he said, and walked on, at an unchanging pace, to the landrovers.

The nearby town of Sodin was a desolate place too. It was market day but many of the stalls were completely bare. Those that were attended had only three or four little piles of goods or spices laid out. The vegetable sellers had built their wares into little piles so sparsely spaced that it was possible to count their entire stock at a glance: one man had for sale 18 little potato-like vegetables. Vultures

stood in rows along the stark branches of the trees above. But at the centre of the market place was the grain bank. This is what they had brought Geldof to see.

That day a meeting had been called to discuss the working of the bank. It had not rained in Sodin for two months and there was going to be nothing to put in the bank from local sources. The town was to meet in committee with the commissioner of the province to discuss the situation. In theory Geldof was to be allowed to observe the meeting; in practice the visit of the Band Aid entourage took over the entire proceeding. From somewhere the townspeople had unearthed a row of large

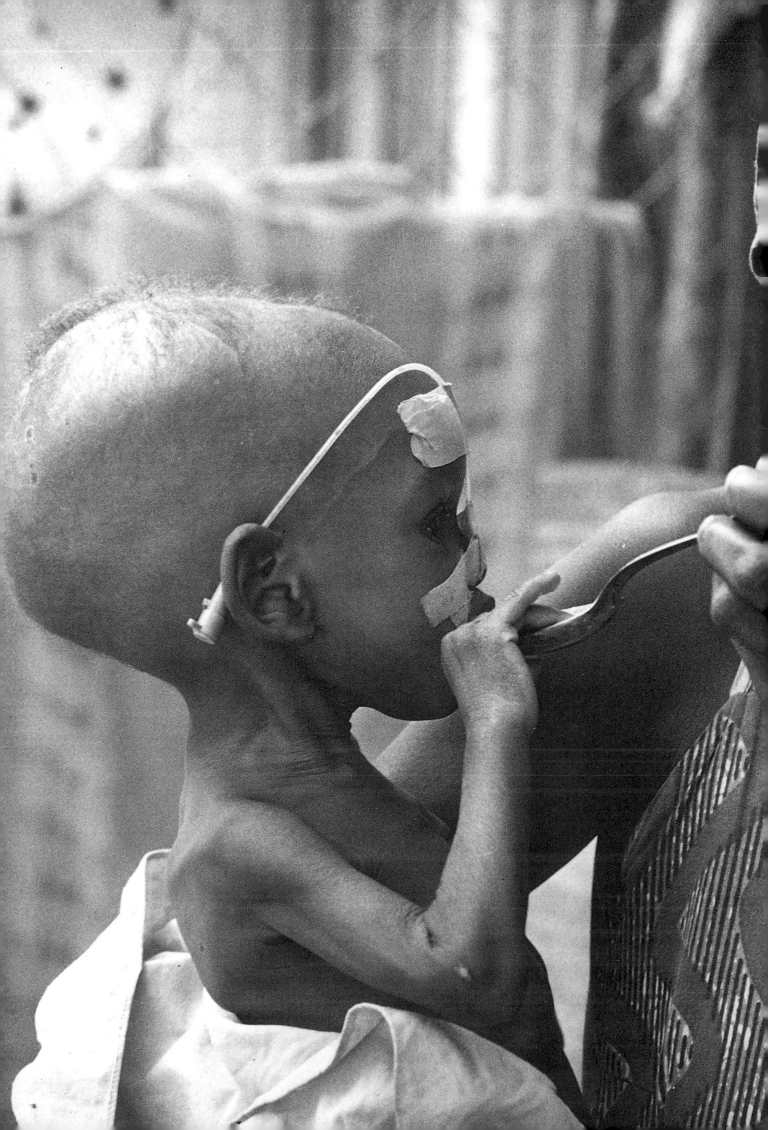

leatherette armchairs which they placed incongruously at the end of an avenue of scrawny trees. About 300 of the local peasants stood, uncomprehending, in a circle around them.

"La patrie ou la mort," shouted the local party cheerleader.

The townsfolk muttered the appropriate response to the beginning of the ideological liturgy.

"Nous vaincrons," roared the party man. The local farmers mumbled their reply without enthusiasm.

Geldof was seated next to the commissioner. A fly-blown aluminium drum was produced. It contained the local sour-tasting millet beer which is served on all important occasions. A large gourd was filled from it and passed along the line of guests. It was preceded by an anxious-looking United Nations official who mumbled to each European, "Just put it to your lips; for God's sake don't drink it."

The beer was passed four more times. Nothing else appeared to be happening.

"I think we're putting a damper on the process of local democracy just by being here. No-one will say anything in front of us. Let's go and look at this f . . . ing grain bank," said Geldof. The town dignitaries, who hadn't been quite sure what to do with him, seemed relieved to see him go. The commissioner followed.

Cereal banks are a comparatively recent invention in Burkina Faso and one that the revolutionary Government has been zealously encouraging through its recently formed Comités de la Défense de la Révolution (CDRs). They deal with a perennial African problem: at harvest time grain prices are low but families are forced to sell their grain to get the cash to pay for taxes and basic household items (often they also have last season's debts to repay); but when their own food stocks run out and they need to buy grain, in the "hungry" season just before the next harvest, prices have risen steeply. The establishment of cereal banks enables village groups to buy grain—normally within the village or locally—when prices are low, and then store it until the hungry season when they sell it to their members at a moderate price. The scheme has many advantages: there are no administrative costs as purchases, supervision and accounting are carried out by unpaid village representatives; transport costs are minimal; it effectively polices the activities of local traders and discourages speculation; local storage avoids the problem of food distribution delays; and, most important, because people can *buy* food through it at a fair price they do not become dependent upon free food nor does an excess of food aid distort the local economy.

The cereal banks, Geldof was told, are funded initially by loans from organizations like Oxfam, but once established they become self-financing. In the first year the bank's committee, elected by the village, is given a small loan to buy grain on a modest scale and is given training sessions. If the first phase is successful the group receives an outright grant to build a simple grain store and a further loan to supplement their revolving fund for grain purchase.

Geldof stood in the Sodin grain bank with bags of free US food aid piled high above his head. Because the harvest here had been non-existent the bank was being stocked with US aid sorghum. Geldof looked around and asked the 'provincial commissioner: "Why is there all this food here when there are people starving in Bogoya just down the road?"

The commissioner launched into a long and complex explanation of the theory of grain banks and the system of food aid distribution. Geldof was unimpressed.

"What I am saying is this: why is that old man dying of hunger in the village over there when there is all this food here?"

By now the commissioner was sweating profusely beneath the combined scrutiny of Geldof and the BBC TV crew who had begun to film the exchange. He wiped his brow, took a quick breath and began to explain the workings of the provincial commission.

"I'm sure the provincial commission is doing its best. But the commission is theoretical; the death is actual. What you're saying is that your system doesn't work."

The commissioner, clutching two ball-point pens in his fist as though they were a mark of office, started to explain the system.

"I'm not interested in the f . . . ing system," Geldof shouted. "Why has he no food? Why is he starving to death?"

This was Geldof at his best, and worst. He has raised more than £50 million to date on little more than a powerful feeling of moral indignation. In Africa he only had to look around him to refuel that sense of outrage. He was in there, as he saw it, as the representative of all the people who had made donations to the Band Aid funds, and he strode around the continent on their behalf, a latterday Everyman, asking the obvious questions which the professionals have forgotten how to ask: "I ask the questions the people who gave the money would ask. If the professionals say they are naive or ill-informed questions, fair enough—just so long as they can give a good answer."

On the other hand, the incident exemplifies Geldof's tendency to respond to complexities by trampling all over them, as he did with the sensibilities of the aid workers in Bogoya village. It is not that he does not understand; merely that he finds it tactically convenient to feign ignorance. He asks for answers but sometimes, if the answers are more complex than he would like to admit, he stops listening and starts on one of his tirades about moral imperatives.

Burkina Faso's revolutionary committees may have failings, but on balance, aid workers from all organizations agree, they are doing remarkably well. Despite ex-ceptions like the one Geldof came across, the cereal bank system seems to work and goes a long way towards controlling the activities of the grain speculators who, until the revolution, used to buy up the harvest at around 30 francs a kilo and resell it seven months later at the height of the dry season for a 400 per cent profit. The CDRs did a magnificent job at the end of 1984 in carrying out a UNICEF vaccination programme in which more than two million children were inoculated against measles, yellow fever and meningitis in only 15 days; until recently Burkina Faso had the highest level of infant mortality in the world, and though it is still high the rate is now falling. The CDRs have also been largely responsible for the work on the 200 dams and on even smaller water-harvesting and anti-erosion projects which have been completed in recent months.

Geldof found his visit to one such dam, being built by peasants just outside Ouahigouya, one of the most heartening experiences of his African tour. It was 450 yards long and 12 feet high and had been built almost entirely by hand. Women with babies fastened to their backs carried the sizeable stones on their heads for up to one and a half miles. The stones were then passed in a human chain to the top of the dam which, the villagers hope, should be finished before the next rainy season. If it is, it will supply water for the farms of more than 5000 people.

"Then there will never be hunger here again," said Ouedraogo Madi, the man elected as foreman by the 600 workers from different villages who have given three days' labour a week for the past four years to the gargantuan project. He was a stocky, muscular man who proudly announced his name was Burkinan for stallion.

"Everyone is helping . . . even the men," he said, and then translated his remark into the local dialect for the chain of women—babies on backs, stones in hand—who worked the side of the dam. They replied with broad grins. One shouted a reply and the women burst into laughter. The foreman shook his fist in mock anger. Their long task was nearly over and they were happy.

"The schoolteachers and trade unionists whom Sankara has locked up in Ouagadougou would not agree but, from this perspective, it has to be said that Sankara's revolution with its anti-bourgeoisie, anti-metropolitan policies is just what an agriculture-based economy like this needs," said one senior UN official.

"It encourages hard work, it discourages dependency on aid and it is not rigidly ideological but fairly pragmatic within its radical populist tradition. If Sankara is not overthrown within the next decade then Burkina Faso could turn itself into a third world model of how even the poorest nation can pull itself up by the sandal straps into some sort of self-sufficiency."

Above top A food store, N'Djamena
outskirts. *Left below* A small gift from
distant parts. *Overleaf* Destitute
peasants, squatting on the outskirts of
N'Djamena.

FACTORS IN THE FAMINE
HOW PEOPLE STARVE TO DEATH

This is what happens when you starve to death.

At first there is hunger and a craving inside which after two or three days turns into a pain. But the obsession with food does not last long. After four or five days the gnawing pains subside and the stomach wall begins to shrink.

Even the thinnest person has, just beneath the skin, layers of subcutaneous fat. At this stage the body begins to live off these fat reserves. How long they will last depends on how healthy you were to start with. If you are an African whose body has been weakened by years of poor diet and intestinal parasites they may last three weeks, or four perhaps. If you are getting a little food, no matter how meagre the supply, this could spin out the whole process for many months.

Eventually, though, your body runs out of fat and begins to live off the substance of the muscles in your thighs, buttocks and upper arms. In a desperate attempt to stay alive you are consuming your own body.

WARNING SYMPTOMS

As if in revolt at this unnatural act, your body erupts in all manner of warning symptoms. Your tongue begins to ache, sores appear at the corners of your mouth, your gums start to bleed or your hands and feet begin to swell. So does your stomach; in children it becomes huge. There may be other signs—a constant buzzing in the ears, headaches, weeping sores, cracked skin.

At this stage the hunger begins to eat into your brain. You have become too tired to work or make much effort to search for food. You have, by now, lost all interest in the idea of food anyway. You become irritable. Occasionally you fly into a real rage, for no reason at all. You find that you are unable to concentrate. You are becoming a different person.

About now, if you are a woman, you stop menstruating. Your body can no longer consider the possibility of reproduction. In any case you long ago lost interest in sex.

Now your hair loses its colour and sheen. It goes soft and falls out in handfuls. Your skin begins to take on a piebald texture. A stranger could now count your every rib from ten yards away. Your upper arms have shrivelled to the width of your forearm, in which you can now see the two bones and the ligaments which join them. Your elbows and wrists stick out like huge comic bulges in comparison. So do your knees, on legs which look like broomsticks covered with skin. Now you really know what is meant by the expression "skin and bone". It is all that you are.

FINAL GRIP

Not that you care much. Your mind has gone past the stage of irritation now. You are overcome with an undefinable sadness. Your eyes have become glazed and a seductive apathy has seeped through every fibre of your body. As starvation takes its final grip you lose interest in everything, even in your own baby who is dying on your lap as you sit, motionless, on the ground.

The aid workers who arrive do not seem to understand this. They keep trying to force you to eat the milky porridge they offer. They keep putting the spoon in your hand and guiding it to the baby's mouth. When they turn their backs to the next sufferer you let it fall from your fingers. It falls to the sand and the flies buzz around; it does not even enter your mind to wave them away. You do not even notice that they are crawling over the baby's eyes and round his face, which is shrivelled like a little monkey's. You sit and stare at nothing. All about you the world goes about its business in some other dimension. You watch through an impenetrable window.

People rarely "starve" to death even in a famine. But the malnutrition lowers their body temperature and increases their vulnerability to "minor" infections which kill.

CHOLERA

Contrary to popular belief, most people in Africa do not die from exotic diseases like yellow fever, sleeping sickness, river blindness, snail fever, or amoebic dysentery. In 1985 in Sudan nearly 2000 people died from cholera in the Ethiopian refugee camps and it made headlines in newspapers throughout the world. Shortly before, 5000 died from measles in the same camps and no-one in the West noticed. In Burkina Faso around half the deaths of children under the age of one are from measles. But, cholera or measles, what they are really dying from is poverty.

More than 13,000 children die in Africa every day. On average 150 in every 1000 die before they reach the age of one, which is 2000 per cent more than in Sweden, Japan or Canada. Those who survive can, on average, expect to be ill for 140 days of the year. They will probably have three or four bouts of diarrhoea, four or five respiratory infections which in the malnourished can turn rapidly to TB, an attack of measles or malaria, plus the usual intestinal parasites and inadequate diet. Many African children are ill nearly all the time.

Safe drinking water and sanitation could cut infant mortality in half. Drinking bad water brings cholera, typhoid, hepatitis, polio and dysentery. Washing in it fosters the spread of eye, skin and intestinal infections. Studies suggest that hand-washing in clean water can reduce childhood illnesses by 40 per cent, yet only five per cent of the population in Ethiopia has access to clean water.

The people of Africa do not need medicine and doctors so much as economic development, clean water schemes, improved food production and distribution and improved education. The tragedy is that Africa today is moving, not towards these goals, but further away from them.

NIGER
The despair of the nomads

About 30 civil servants had turned up in a huge air-conditioned bus to meet Bob Geldof as he arrived at Agadez, and quite clearly they were disappointed. The night before, he had been interviewed by Niger's national television station which had dubbed him, without any trace of irony, Geldof d'Afrique. Now here he was shambling from the executive jet with a total lack of ceremony. He was wearing his yellow boots with black skull and crossbones emblems and a faded blue shirt unfastened at the sleeves, and his long hair hung in unkempt ringlets like the fleece of a mangy desert goat. Worse than that, he had not brought the Minister.

The civil servants, dressed in their Friday finery, were spruced up for the unaccustomed honour of meeting the Minister of Health. Many of them had travelled hundreds of miles from their various far-flung outposts for the occasion. It is rare that a provincial civil servant gets the chance to meet and, hopefully, impress the Minister himself. They had waited at the tiny airport with great expectations. But the man himself did not turn up, only the pop singer from England. From now on the whole thing would be rather a waste of time. They settled themselves ungraciously into the high-wheeled coach with its ice-cold air conditioning on full and began to dispense amongst themselves chilled Coke and beer from their massive cold box.

They could hide neither their impatience nor their bewilderment when, within minutes, the Band Aid party ordered the bus to a halt by the market in

Right **Leaving the Presidential Palace, Khartoum.** *Overleaf* **Geldof sleeps on the aid grain being flown into El Geneina, Sudan.**

the centre of the oasis town. Geldof had left behind in the hotel in the capital, Niamey, the white headdress he had been given in Timbuctoo to protect him from the fierce Sahara sun. He needed another.

The market came to a standstill. Groups of superior merchants broke off from the formalities of conversation with which they preceded their complex deals and spoke in furtive asides as they inspected the crocodile of white men which descended from the bus and wound its way through the labyrinth of stalls. Women shopping for food lifted their veils even higher or turned their heads demurely. Tall, silent Berbers, in the black and white robes of visitors from the desert, stood stock still and watched, their swathes of headgear revealing only their eyes and their eyes revealing only disdain for these ill-clothed little foreigners.

It was a fine market, a hundred times the size of the miserable affair in Timbuctoo only a few days before, for Agadez was still a commercial centre of significance. Different sections of the souk specialized in different produce. Geldof was guided to the covered stalls which sold cloth. This time he stood and said little as El Hadji, a real expert, did the bargaining.

El Hadji was a small man but seemed to lose no respect on account of that; but then, as his very name implied, he commanded deference because in better days he had made the Hadj, the pilgrimage to Mecca. Time was, he told Geldof later, when Agadez was full of men entitled to the appellation. But then, as times got harder for even the merchant class and the cost of overland travel to the Red Sea and then a passage across to the holy city became even more expensive, the Hadjij in Agadez became an increasingly exclusive brotherhood. He smiled engagingly, revealing a broken tooth.

"He is an amazing character. When we arrived he just attached himself to us. He organizes everything. We'd be absolutely lost without him. Yet he never asks for anything. For him it is an honour to help us," explained Diane Hanson, who with her husband Tony runs 22 Red Cross feeding stations in the Agadez area.

El Hadji bargained for three Tuareg headdresses, long fine cotton wraps which appeared black from a distance but close to could be seen to be a deep purple, dyed with an inky indigo which left the fingers dark from handling the cloth. Back on the bus the old Arab draped it carefully around Geldof's head, at first in the traditional manner, leaving the crown exposed, and then later enveloping the singer in a cloud of purple so that only his mischievous eyes showed.

The settlement selected for us by the Hansons was a 35-mile drive out of Agadez. The landscape through which the coach sped along a surprisingly good road was a flat, sterile plain of dust with only the occasional euphobia bush to break the monotony. Throughout this semi-desert Sahelian region, which runs across Africa

along the belly of the Sahara proper, this shrub is to be found, extracting moisture from the arid sand where no other plant can survive. It has broad succulent leaves which exude a luxurious white sap when broken open. It looks an admirable source of water but it is, as Geldof puts it, "another of God's little jokes"—the sap is deadly poisonous and just a spot of it in the eye can make a man go blind. Once, at this time of year, there would have been sabay here, a grain that grows wild on the fertile margins of the desert. Now there was none. Apart from the euphobia there was

nothing; only the unending greyness of the sands which stretched to the horizon and blended in a heat haze with the thin blue of the sky. This, ecologists had told us in advance, was what we should expect in the area north of 15 degrees latitude. It is unfortunate for Niger that a good 80 per cent of its land surface lies north of that.

After the temperate air of the coach the heat hit Geldof like a physical blow when he stepped out onto the sand.

"This is one of the most hostile places I have ever been in my life," he said with genuine awe.

Food aid arrives in the remote west of Sudan on a Danish airforce Transall as part of the EEC airlift. It is unloaded straight onto the Oxfam lorry by local labourers.

Within seconds the beads of sweat began to appear on his brow. They were aggravated by the presence of the brigade of bureaucrats who descended from the coach and surrounded him. It was as if they wanted to keep a protective barrier between the rock star and reality. Geldof and his human armour moved slowly off

towards the nearest group of nomads.

They called it a settlement. They had even given the place the glamour of a name — Tiguerouit. The idea seemed an absurdity for, at first glance, there was nothing to distinguish the spot from the boundless desolation which lay before us. What there was, it transpired, was a borehole which the local people had, with foreign aid, dug themselves a year earlier. But from afar there had been no sign of its presence, only the limitless sand and the nomads' shelters — domed structures of white linen or raffia mats stretched over a

few bent poles. Around lay the sun-dried carcasses of beasts that had perished in this year of drought which is without parallel since the beginning of the century.

They were a mixed group of settlers: Fulani peoples who traditionally are cattle herders and Tuaregs from further north whose livestock is normally camels. But traditional differences had no place among the nomads of Tiguerouit. They were united by the fact that, without a single exception, all their animals were dead.

Geldof was getting impatient with the massed bands of official guards. He strode purposefully through them to the place where the meagre rations of food were being distributed and beyond to a group of dark-robed women who were regarding him with undisguised curiosity. Perhaps, even, they were eyeing him up. For although Geldof did not know it these were the women of the Peul Borourou whose sexual liberality has delighted generations of Western anthropologists.

Among this tribe it is the women who take the sexual initiatives. They choose their husbands during an annual ritual dance in which the men cavort with much rolling of the eyeballs and baring of the teeth, for with these Fulani the whiteness of the teeth and eyes are the greatest marks of beauty. And if a Peul Borourou husband should come home and find another man's sandals outside his tent he will turn meekly away and wait until the interloper has been dismissed. If the woman wants to make the new arrangement permanent she will disappear into the desert with her new lover for five weeks until her passion is spent. Then she will return with the new man in tow and from that point on they will be accepted by the rest of the tribe as a married couple.

They were proud women, with rather broad features for desert folk and ritual scars on their cheeks. Their faces were not covered and they returned Geldof's stare, unflinching even when he turned the ubiquitous home video camera on them. He smiled and nodded and, unaware of how close he might have come to being acquired, moved on to a dried-out patch of millet and sorghum plants.

Throughout Niger there are 913 settlements like this for destitute nomads. There are close on a million people who have lost all their livestock in the past year's drought. About 300,000 of them have simply moved south and formed primitive squats on the edge of the country's main towns where they live as beggars and scavengers. There are so many of these shanty towns, that their occupants often outnumber the residents of the original towns. But there have also been moves to settle as many as 400,000 of these nomadic refugees in places where they can be encouraged to supplement their food aid with a little farming in what the Government calls contre-saison projects.

At Tiguerouit there have been such attempts, as one particular peasant was anxious to demonstrate. As Geldof approached her minuscule plot the stately little woman held out her hands and cried out in Hausa.

"She is saying: 'See. The hands of a Fulani woman. The hands of a Fulani should be like silk. See. Feel these hands,'" translated Diane Hanson who, despite the fact that she slinks around the

Geldof with Chadian refugees at Azernay, western Sudan. This is the image he tries to avoid. He finds it uncomfortable.

camp in chic designer spectacles with a smart handbag slung over her shoulder, has lived in Niger for three years and speaks the local language with admirable fluency.

The woman stretched out her hands still further to display the roughened skin and callouses. Her name was Guntu Mamane and for the past 50 years she had wandered the Sahara with her small tribe, living off the milk of her cattle and goats with a little wild honey when she could find it or a small amount of grain when she could trade it. But last year she lost eight head of cattle, two donkeys, eight goats and eight sheep.

She counted them off on her blistered fingers. Since then she had been forced for the first time in 50 years to use a hoe.

"I had nothing to live on and I had two children to look after. I am married to an old man who cannot see and has no teeth," she said dismissively, as though the lack of teeth was somehow deliberate. "I have to give him food and clothes too," she added with cold charity.

"Look at my crop."

Geldof went and peered down Guntu's well and then looked at the brown and broken plants. Many times a day, she said, she drew the water and poured it carefully around the stems of the dozen rows of millet and sorghum she had planted. But the crop was not a good one.

In the shade the temperature would have been 115 degrees F, but here there was no shade. The ground soaked up the water so rapidly that within a few minutes it looked as if the soil had never been moistened at all.

Still, she explained, because she had a good supply of water she did not have to wait for another season to try again. She would plant again next month and hope that the sun would be less fierce and her plants would prosper. She had had some luck in the past and had saved enough, because of the high price of grain and by doing a little work for the Red Cross, to buy two new goats. She would carry on planting until two had by multiplication become three and she had earned enough from selling her grain to buy enough beasts to form a viable herd. Then, as her ancestors had done before her, she would move on.

Geldof took his cue from the remark and pressed his way through the tightening ring of government officials and bolted across the compacted sands, his turban fluttering in the slight breeze, his ever-present video camera over his shoulder. A few brave bureaucrats made an attempt to follow him but it was much too hot for such foolishness. They left him to it and began to mill around the coach and press for a return to air conditioning and civilization. Diane Hanson, meanwhile, continued her watchful tour of the camp.

"Of course what we can do here is very limited but it does offer a solution to a number of the local problems," she said. "For a start it has kept people out here in the desert which has been their home for centuries instead of congregating uselessly in towns. It also goes a step beyond the straightforward feeding of the starving. Some of those working here now are

people we found collapsed in the desert six months ago; now they not only have food but some little hope for the future. It is a small contribution to the revegetation of the desert margins. And it could form the basis of a return to their old way of life; as they make some money they can start to rebuild their herds and then send their children off with the animals to look for grazing while the parents stay here and cultivate."

Back on the bus the Nigerien civil service was getting edgy. Lunchtime was drawing dangerously close and we had a 35-mile drive back to the official banquet they were anticipating.

But where was Geldof?

It was another 20 minutes before he emerged from the tent of one of the nomad chiefs. He looked pleased with himself. The conversation had been limited but it had been totally free of the official translatorese which he was now starting to find really irksome. It had been hot inside and the sweat on his forehead had mingled with the indigo dye in his headcloth and streaked his cheeks with woad like some ancient British chieftain. "They will have been pleased at that," said Diane. "Among the Tuareg the blue dye on the face is a mark of great distinction. It shows

that you can afford good quality cloth."

He had not been aboard the coach for ten minutes when he spotted two sizeable herds of camels and cattle mingling around a water hole a few hundred yards from the road.

"I thought they were all supposed to be dead," cried Geldof. "Stop the bus. I want to have a look. Stop the bus."

They stopped the bus. To the horror of the majority of its passengers Geldof clambered down and wandered into the desert. Behind him rows of hungry faces gazed with disbelief from the windows of the coach as Geldof turned his video camera on the animals.

The beasts, which waited without any such sense of urgency by the well, looked healthy enough. The long-horned African cattle were well-fleshed and the camels, even those still waiting for the borehole's donkey to draw the water from the 60-metre-deep well, looked plump-bellied.

"They are doing fine," said Tony Hanson. "Those animals which did survive have little competition for grazing now." Most of the livestock that died did so from lack of grazing rather than thirst.

"How did these survive, then?" asked Geldof.

Hanson turned and spoke in Hausa to El Hadji who, in turn, spoke in an even more obscure language to the blue-veiled Tuareg who was dividing the camels into smaller groups as they approached the well. The process of translation and re-translation seemed endless. It was like listening to a verbal tennis match without having the rules explained. Somehow it was an apt metaphor for the labyrinthine processes which dog all foreign aid de-

velopment in Africa. But eventually an answer did emerge.

"These beasts were sold early in the drought to rich townspeople who could afford to move them south to better pasture. Now the townsmen have hired their former owners to look after them. Eventually they hope, through their wages, to be able to buy them back."

"But, of course, they sold when livestock was worth little and now it is in great demand and the price is high," said Geldof.

"Of course."

Some of the nomads had actually bought their animals back already. But to do so they had had to go into enormous debt.

Geldof wandered through the herds of animals. As he did so two small boys approached. From little paper bags they took some objects and held them out on the outstretched palms of their hands for his inspection. They were tiny flint arrowheads. The boys passed the time by searching for them in the hot sands. Geldof took one from each boy and gave them the smallest note of Nigerien currency from his pocket. Their eyes widened. It was worth only about one pound sterling but it was clearly more than they had ever before possessed.

Geldof carefully placed the little arrowheads on his own palm and gazed at them. They were all that now survived from the time of the lush forests in which local hunters with their bows had searched for the plentiful game which inhabited them. The arrowheads were from a period of prehistory, perhaps 20,000 years ago, El

Above A crop of sorghum that failed. A few miles away (*Right*) a crop flourishes. Rainfall in the desert is very localized. Near El Geneina, Western Sudan. *Overleaf* Digging for water in a dried-up river bed outside El Geneina, western Sudan.

Hadji said through Diane Hanson. The sad thing was that the same forests could have been there a mere 100 years ago, so much had the land around Agadez altered in that short time.

Back in the town, lunch was in the cramped little restaurant owned by El Hadji. The civil servants were furious. They had hoped the Red Cross would lay on a grand banquet in some official residence. Geldof, after days of eating only hotel food, was happy enough with the dark little eating house and its local cuisine, but the bureaucrats were insulted. They vented their spleen by descending upon the two whole sheep which El Hadji's cooks brought in and ripping them apart with their bare hands in an undisguised display of greed.

Geldof sat patiently and waited until they had finished. The bellies of the beasts had been stuffed with beans and a spicy couscous so there was, in the event, plenty left.

In Niger, as in every country affected by the famine in Africa, it is rarely the civil servants who go hungry.

All over Africa they congregate in the capital cities and main towns and nurture their bureaucracy, draining wealth away from the rural areas of production. What was quickly becoming clear to Geldof was that, great though the contrasts are bet-

ween the lifestyles of the West and the third world, there is just as disturbing a contrast between the rural peasants in Africa and the elites in the capital cities who rule them. Geldof knew he would soon be returning to all that, to the Nigerien capital, Niamey, and its great tower blocks of ministerial offices with their leather armchairs and their billowing lace curtains, its prestigious and usually empty national museum, its well-stocked shops, its restaurants full of imported French wines and cheeses, and a modern hotel so luxurious and outrageously expensive that it charged more than $40 for a wrong-number telephone call.

But before the flight back to Niamey Geldof had to pay a courtesy call on the préfet of this town of the nomads.

"F . . . ing protocol," he said when the government man from the capital insisted it was, along with a ration of local dancing, obligatory. At the entrance to the low brick building with its atmosphere of a pre-war primary school Geldof paused, like a reluctant schoolboy dragging his feet, and exploited the excuse of talking to a group of young Americans who were in the town as Peace Corps volunteers.

The government man was getting anxious.

"What exactly do you do here?" Geldof asked them, beginning to sound dangerously like Prince Charles.

The government man looked irritably at his watch.

Most had predictable enough occupations, teaching in the local school, working on the town's health projects. But one gangling youth managed the not inconsiderable feat of silencing the garrulous Irishman.

"I'm here to teach them to play basketball."

There was no answer to that, though Geldof, recalling the incident later that night in the bar of the Gaweye Hotel in Niamey, eventually managed to come up with an unprintable one. But in Agadez he was speechless, and allowed himself to be shepherded into the Bureau du Préfet by a triumphant government man.

Once inside, the tone changed. The préfet was a tall and quietly spoken man who talked with dignity of the problems of his people.

"They are suffering from want of water. That is the basic problem still. We have had some rains, yet strangely the water table has not risen and remains at the level it has held since the early days of the drought. We are now having to dig deeper and deeper for water—60 metres, 150 metres, even 200 metres. We know that the water is there but it is at great depths. To us this is an insuperable problem. To Western technology it is the work of minutes."

Geldof nodded his silent assent, picking up more of the préfet's French than he had led people to believe he could understand.

"Now we have something we should like to give you," the préfet said as the Band Aid party stood on the steps of his office ready to depart. The head of the municipality made a signal to one of his aides who appeared from behind a nearby door bearing a most handsome hand-tooled leather camel saddle.

"It is a Tuareg saddle. This is a great honour," whispered one of the aid workers.

"Take this as a token of all you have done for our people," said the préfet with simple ceremony.

Geldof's eyes filled with a sadness. It did not seem proper to take something so fine from a people who had so little. It did not seem proper to refuse.

"Remember this," said the préfet. "When you get home to England your wife and child will be there to greet you. If they had gone away there would be a great emptiness in your house. You would miss the sound of their presence, their footsteps, their talking.

"So tell the people of Europe this. My people here in Agadez, they are the children of the developed world. If you let them die the whole world will feel the great emptiness. You will miss the sound of our crying."

CHAD
The spoils of war

Geldof wanted to go for a swim. It was very hot. He had survived for a week on four hours' sleep a night. At the best of times he is not a figure of sartorial elegance. Now he looked terrible. He sprouted stubble like a young Yasser Arafat. His eyes were hollow. He had not once sat in the sun and was developing an unhealthy pallor. His big toe hurt. The toe-nail had started growing in and was beginning to turn septic. This is a very minor complaint in the context of Central Africa, where yellow fever, river blindness and cerebral malaria are major health hazards, and Geldof got scant sympathy, especially from Jenden, who had an abcess on his thigh which was dangerously poisoned and very painful.

"God my toe hurts," Geldof said.

"Don't tell me about your toe, Geldof, I think my leg's gone gangrenous," said Jenden.

"Stop making a fuss about a spot on your leg, Jenden," said Geldof.

Vallely had vomited that morning in an insalubrious lavatory at the airport. Herrmann felt sick. Blundy and Morris had streaming colds brought on by the constant changes from air conditioning in the capitals to fierce heat in the provinces. Morris had difficulty putting over his TV and radio broadcasts because his voice had degenerated into a husky whisper.

This rancid-looking group had shuffled out of the BA 125 that morning at N'Djamena airport in Chad, in the very heart of Africa. Because of Geldof's obsession about protocol our reception had been cut to the minimum. No little singers of the raised fist or doves of the revolution greeted us on the tarmac. Just a couple of Chadian officials and the aid worker from the Red Cross who organized the trip.

Geldof, wearing his bathing trunks and holding a towel, limped through the foyer of the Chadienne Hotel and out the back to the pool, crossing a concrete platform where local people laid out souvenirs and knick-knacks carved from wood and shells. He went to the edge of the pool. It was a third full of green slime. It looked as if it had not been cleaned or emptied since the civil war in 1982. Malarial mosquitoes swarmed above it, forming a thin mist. Bugs and other small creatures skidded over the surface. Organic substances deep in the slime seethed, sending bursts of bubbles to the surface.

"It's like the primordial soup," said Geldof.

"It's like an experiment Frankenstein half finished," said Jenden.

Above left **Even in the dry season transport lorries get stuck in the sand. Food aid is off-loaded to free the lorry.** *Above* **Aid workers digging out Geldof's landrover.** *Overleaf* **Wad Sherifay, the biggest refugee camp in Sudan and the country's third largest "city". Current official population: 185,000 Eritreans, fled from the war in Ethiopia.**

The stall holders had stood up to watch this long-haired, spindly white man in bathing trunks commit suicide by plunging in. Geldof disappointed them. He backed away and we walked towards the banks of the Chari River. The ground seemed to move under our feet as millions of tiny grasshoppers jumped in unison out of our way. We all remembered Geldof's awful warning about grasshoppers. We turned and headed for the bar.

The principle that has sustained Geldof during a frantic year of fund raising is that everything is possible if you have the will and the energy. People can be persuaded to give money, governments forced by moral pressure to give aid and to change their policies. It is a principle which in 1985 has saved many thousands of lives in Africa. The problems facing Chad are so vast, however, that even Geldof's spirits began to flag.

The centre of N'Djamena looks like Beirut does after 11 years of the Lebanese

civil war. Yet N'Djamena's battle dates back only to 1982. The Government's coffers are so bare that next to nothing has been done to repair the damage caused by civil war which raged, briefly, in the capital. The main street, Avenue Charles de Gaulle, is broad and impressive, absurdly so as only a few Chadians can afford cars and there is almost no fuel. The petrol stations are mostly closed. There are now stalls by the side of the road selling wine, beer and soft-drink bottles—all full of the same yellow liquid. It is petrol, which drivers buy literally by the bottle and pour into their tanks. The buildings along this magnificent boulevard are shattered, pock-marked by bullets and with gaping holes from heavy artillery shells. Few buildings are unscathed. The front of the cathedral still stands, a towering arch with a round window. The rest of it has been completely destroyed. It is now like a piece of stage scenery.

There has been drought and famine in Chad for ten years. Last summer the drought was so bad that 128,000 people flocked from the countryside towards N'Djamena in search of food. To stop the capital being flooded with refugees who were on the point of causing another civil war, the Government introduced "Operation Wall", a ring of camps around the city to hold the famine victims. Thousands of them died.

Since that time it has rained, but the rain brought its own problems. The great Logone and Chari Rivers, which had been reduced to a trickle, suddenly flooded, destroying crops and villages, and spreading disease. Apart from warning about the rats and the rabies, the UN now advises

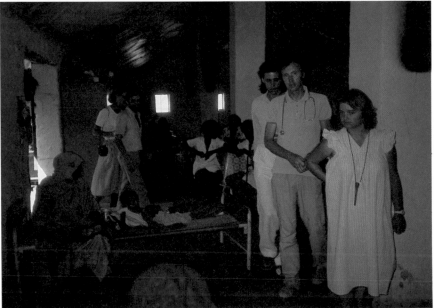

visitors to avoid local milk products, leafy vegetables and tapwater, which was not a problem in the Chadienne Hotel because there was no running water. It advises them to take malaria suppressant drugs, and have shots for hepatitis, typhoid, cholera and yellow fever.

Despite the rains, about a quarter of Chad's five million people are affected by famine. Many were too weak to plant seeds this year. The seed itself was often bad and failed to grow. The rain, for which people had prayed for so long, washed the seed or the crops away.

The main victims of famine are the children. A third of the nation's children do not have enough to eat. A third suffer

Top Hospital ward at Wad Sherifay. A model of its kind. *Above* Geldof touring the wards with Swiss Red Cross doctors and nurses. *Right* Waiting beneath the surgery sign for treatment. *Overleaf* A few lucky refugees can find work in the camp hospital.

from anaemia. If they survive childhood their life expectancy is, according to the United Nations statistics, only 43 years, one of the lowest in the world. Only 15 per cent of all the people in Chad can read or write. There is one doctor for every 47,000 people. The economy is declining at a rate of 2.2 per cent a year. This makes it, after Bhutan, the poorest, most unfor-

CHILDRENS HOSPITAL

S R C

WAD SHERIFAY

Above **Food storage depot at Wad Sherifay, Sudan.**
Right **A meeting at Wad Sherifay.**

tunate country in the world. And if that were not enough, it is also a country racked by civil war.

We all sat at tables near the foetid pool of the Chadienne to be briefed by aid workers and diplomats, pale, thin, sickly people who had lived in Chad, in some cases for years, and had all succumbed to the illnesses that prevail there. They are courageous. "When I meet people like that I feel pathetic. I feel I haven't done a thing. I don't think I could face it, the sickness, the misery, month after month," said Geldof.

It was the gloomiest briefing of the trip. Our combined knowledge of the political intricacies of Chad was flimsy. On the plane from Niger, and in the hotel, we had pored over the background material on a country beset by coups and countercoups, with two separate civil wars, one in the north and one in the south.

"It's a mess," said Geldof.

"It surely is," said a lady from the US embassy.

Geldof had heard a story, but could not remember quite where, that the President of Chad, Hissein Habre, had personally executed two prisoners when he had been a rebel leader in the 70s. The men had been condemned to death, Geldof had heard, and Habre had gone down to the cells and strangled them.

"Come off it, Bob," said one of us. "That's like the story about the grasshoppers with AIDS."

"I swear it's true," said Geldof. "How would I know that about him going down in the cells if I hadn't read it?"

Geldof said he would ask the President next day when we had an audience. "Go ahead," said Jenden. "You'll be the third victim."

In the context of Chad's bloody recent history, a strangling or two seems a small matter. President Habre used to be a rebel leader fighting against the present rebel leader, Goukouni Oueddei, who was at that time the President. The plot thickens. Both Habre and Oueddei were friends and allies in the 70s and helped depose Francois Tombalbaye, who was the first President after independence from France in 1960, and the next President, General Felix Malloum. Oueddei then became President and Habre was his Minister of Defence.

"So who did all this then?" said Geldof, pointing to the line of bullet holes stitched across the back wall of the hotel. "Was that Tombalwhatsit or what?"

"No, it was not," said the lady from the American embassy. She explained that the city was devastated in 1980, when Habre unsuccessfully attacked the forces of his old friend President Oueddei, and again in 1982, when Habre's men took the town and gained control. Habre became President. Oueddei fled north, where, with Libyan help, he remains.

"His followers are called the Gunt," said the lady diplomat.

"You're joking," said Geldof.

"No, that's their name. G-U-N-T. Really."

The country was split in two and both Habre and Oueddei claimed to be the legitimate rulers. The north, or Oueddei's kingdom, is now virtually a department of Libya. The northern capital, Faya Largeau, flies the Libyan flag, has a Libyan prefect and 5000 Libyan troops. Habre also faces an entirely separate rebellion in the south. Most of his time, effort and budget is spent fighting on two fronts.

There is a real fear in N'Djamena that the Libyans will move south and take the whole country. A few days before, a Libyan Tupolev bomber had made several passes over the city. People had fled from the streets and taken cover, expecting the bombs to rain down. In fact the plane appeared to have been on a reconnaissance run. This event did little to repair the frayed nerves of N'Djamenans. During our brief stay, there would be unconfirmed reports of two attacks by Libyan fighter planes just north of the capital.

The Chadians feel strongly that they have been sold down the Chari River by the French, and by the Americans. They are especially bitter about the French. The best-selling book in the Al Akhbar book shop in N'Djamena is *Operation Manta* by a French army colonel called Spartacus. It describes how the French betrayed their former colony. It was the anniversary of the great betrayal, as the locals call it, and they talked of little else in the bar of the Chadienne that evening. In 1983 Oueddei launched, with massive Libyan military assistance, an attack on the north. He took Faya Largeau and was moving rapidly south towards N'Djamena. After fierce prompting by the US, the French moved in to support Habre. The Oueddei attack was halted.

Top Arriving at Port Sudan. *Right* On the dock at Port Sudan where the nine Band Aid ships arrive. *Overleaf* Discussions at UNICEF headquarters, Port Sudan.

Hundreds of French soldiers were based in N'Djamena. The locals recall their packing the bar of the Chadienne, and how some of them, intoxicated by drink and the admiring looks of the local ladies of the night, plunged where Geldof did not dare, into the foetid pool. The soldiers carried back to France stories of their daring deeds, plus doses of hepatitis, dysentery and some virulent types of venereal disease.

A year ago the French did a deal with Libya. They agreed to withdraw, simultaneously, from Chad, leaving it under the control of President Habre. The French withdrew promptly. The Libyans stayed on. Habre still only ruled half the country. Neither the French nor the Americans are willing to help Habre retake the north. "We are not going to war with Libya, and that is that," said a French diplomat.

During our journey through the Sahel Geldof had been optimistic. In Mali, Burkina, Niger there was suffering and appalling deprivation, but there was also hope that conditions would improve. The international aid, and Band Aid's contribution to it, would go towards long-term development in an attempt to ensure that the horrors of the 1985 drought did not occur again. Even in the ravaged wastes of northern Mali we had seen the rice paddy project which could be used to keep the population of Timbuctoo alive.

By comparison Chad was a nightmare. "How can you plan long-term when you've got two civil wars, Libyan bombers buzzing around, drought, disease and no money?" said Geldof. Earlier that day he had visited the hospital in N'Djamena. It is one of the best medical centres in a country where most people have no doctors or medicine. The conditions were appalling. It was so overcrowded that children slept two or three in a bed. Others lay on the floor underneath the beds and in the corridor. There was a crust of blood on the floor and no running water except for a dribble of brown, viscous liquid that flowed down the side of one ward. It was a sewer, running from the lavatory. As Jenden left the hospital dusk was falling and the power supply had failed once again. There were tears in his eyes. "What this sums up is the disaster of under-development even without the famine. For Christ's sake, this is the national hospital!" He was not without knowledge of how such places should be. After the famine in Ethiopia in the mid 70s he spent some time as an architect with the Red

Cross designing medical buildings.

Aid workers and Government representatives in N'Djamena had assured Geldof that the famine in Chad was over. The problems were now, as in the other Sahel countries, the casualties of the famine: the dispossessed and the displaced.

This official version did not prepare Geldof for the eerie and terrible scene he witnessed near Bukoro, a village 100 miles from the capital on the second day of our visit. There he was taken to see two camps in "Operation Wall", the cordon sanitaire around N'Djamena. The first one,

Tchawaze, wasn't bad. There, nomads had been given seeds and tools and taught how to plant a crop. It had worked to a large extent. Rains had been adequate and early plantings were already bearing a good crop, although the dreaded grasshoppers had eaten a quarter of it. The number of children who were severely malnourished had dropped from 2000 to 200 thanks to food aid and the early harvest. Aid workers thought that their help would not be needed in this camp by early 1986.

But in the second, a dry and nameless

place the project had been an utter failure.

When the landrover pulled up in the small cluster of trees which was all that distinguished the place from the vast expanse of dry savannah which stretched between there and N'Djamena, hundreds of people moved from the shade of the boughs beneath which they were sheltering from the 115 degrees F heat. There were no houses here, no shelters, no tents—nothing except the stultified people beneath the trees.

It was not the sort of crowd Bob Geldof was used to having surround him. Nor was

it the sort which he had expected to find in a country where everyone in the capital had told him the famine was over.

The men approached first, cautiously. Then from within their ranks appeared women, steering children before them. They stood in a tight semi-circle around Geldof and Jenden. Nothing was said. But quietly, and all at once as if by some prearranged signal, the women began slowly to remove the children's clothes.

"It was not a new sight," Geldof said later, recalling the incident with dismay. "It was a sight I had seen before in Ethiopia and Sudan. But, for me, it is a sight it is impossible to get used to."

The children stood there naked, like tiny old men and women. They too made not a sound. Geldof said nothing. The silence was unnatural but these children were beyond words. They stood there and stared, uncomprehending. Their eye sockets were sunken. Their rib cages protruded painfully through their skin. Their huge elbows stood in bulges, like deformed growths, from their scrawny little arms. Their legs were as thin as sticks. The children of famine, still.

Continuing the speechless conversation the men came forward bearing samples of this year's crop—sticks of millet, eaten in the bud by caterpillars, and heads of dusty sorghum.

"God's cruellest trick: a first rain to germinate the seeds, a second rain to bring to crop to full height, but no third rain to fill the empty husks," Geldof was later to describe it. But before these people he could find no words.

One farmer crumbled the crop between his fingers, and the grain, infested by a carbon weevil, turned to a fine black powder. The hand continued, remorselessly, until the whole head of cereal disappeared into soot and was swirled into the air by little eddies of wind.

The nomads, whose families had for centuries lived only on animal products, had had the most dispiriting introduction to agriculture.

"The rains were poor and the people farmed badly. An experienced farmer could just have got a crop here but these people did not clear the ground adequately and we could not make them understand the need to keep the land completely free of weeds," said Ramadan Hussein, an official of the Government's agricultural department.

The nomads were perplexed by the criticism.

"To use the hoe was difficult. It is not a natural movement for a herdsman," said one of them, Albayan Abduli, swaying in clumsy demonstration. He had had 70 cattle before the drought.

"We tried to clear the weeds but still we got no crop," said Sale Ali, who had travelled 800 miles from Tibesti and lost his entire herd of 400 camels in the process.

"This is all we got," said Sale Muza, waving the forlorn husks. Once, in Oum Hadjer, he had owned 70 camels, 100 cows and 40 goats. Now he had nothing.

It had been a bad and depressing day. Geldof was in no mood for the good news which the lady from the American embassy brought to the Chadienne Hotel. He and Jenden had been given an award by the President of the United States. The

Above & right **A shanty town, home for nearly half a million people, built on a rubbish dump on the outskirts of Port Sudan.** *Overleaf* **Band Aid in action: Geldof with some of the seventy lorries Band Aid uses to ferry food from Port Sudan.**

President wanted to speak to them both personally on the phone later that day. They could not have been less excited if they had received an early-morning wake-up call.

"Well, OK, that's very nice. I'm not sure how we can take the call," said Geldof.

"What is the award?" said Jenden. The lady from the embassy was not sure, but she was sure that it was very special and a great honour.

Geldof said later that he hadn't meant to seem impolite. "It's just that today was shocking. I have seen that kind of suffering before but, I suppose, after those optimistic reports we heard from the Government, I didn't expect to see those kids. They were starving. Christ. Sometimes the enormity of this problem is shattering. It's not that me and Kevin aren't flattered by an award. It's just that in this context, here in Chad, it seems so irrelevant." He would say to Morris on a BBC film that was shown on the American network NBC next day that next year President Reagan should triple US international aid and give himself the award. For once, though, Geldof was being the diplomat. "That doesn't sound churlish, does it?" he asked Morris.

"No, it's OK," said Morris.

"Are you sure?" said Geldof.

The US State Department had telexed information about the award and signed it "Thank you, Shultz". If the US Secretary of State, George Shultz, was sending information telexes to the embassy in Chad this must be a very big deal indeed. The telex said that this was the third annual Presidential World Without Hunger Award. The presentation would be held next day in Washington, when Geldof would be in mid-air heading for Sudan. The award criteria took up a whole page of telex: "the nominee will be measured as follows: achievement of specific goals

Above **The Band Aid lorries leave for the 2½ day drive to Khartoum. Among them are the lorries people said would never work. Band Aid bought forty second-hand vehicles that the other aid agencies in Sudan would not touch.**
Right **One of the thirty new lorries shipped from Kuwait. Every truck carries the Band Aid symbol—taken by some locals to mean "Let's Eat Africa".**

leading to the solution of the problem of hunger, including services rendered and people affected, the development and promotion of individual initiative in the third world, creative efforts to increase public awareness of the underlying problems of world hunger," and so on.

We went along to the embassy at eight that evening. It is a heavily fortified building, like all US embassies in trouble spots. American marines searched each car as it entered and pushed a trolley, with a mirror on it, under the car to search for bombs. They had a device for sniffing explosives and a chicane of concrete to deter the suicide bomber. Inside we sat in a room next to the embassy security headquarters, a small box encased in bullet-proof glass which contains an armoury of automatic rifles and shot guns, and banks of television screens which scan the inside and outside of the building. We were late. The State Department had called from Washington, prepared to patch the call through to the White House. They had hung on for half an hour, then hung up. They would call back. We waited for 40 minutes. Geldof grew restless.

"I hope they can get through quicker than this if there's a war or something," said Geldof.

"We have a momentary communication problem that I am sure will be resolved," said an embassy official.

In the end Geldof said, "I'm sorry, we've got to go and have dinner with these Ministers." The call came a few minutes after we had left. The State Department and the White House switchboard hung on while the embassy sent out envoys in fruitless pursuit.

Dinner was in the Hotel Chari, the finest restaurant in town. It has a style bequeathed by French-colonial rule. The waiters were smartly turned out in black uniforms, the table cloths were clean and white. The menu had fine food cooked with French delicacy and flair and good vintage wine imported from France. There was even imported ice cream. Appetites were blunted however by the scene that greeted guests in the hotel entrance. As our landrovers pulled up outside, a dozen beggars in battered wheelchairs sped towards us and formed up in a rank before the hotel steps. Many had no legs. Others were hideously deformed by war or nature. They stay in the hotel entrance every day and most of the night, hoping to pick up a few coins. Every city has its disparities between rich and poor. Manhattan has the most expensive real estate and the richest people in the world only a few blocks from the poverty and deprivation of Harlem. In Chad, though, the contrast was starker and more shocking.

Geldof picked at his boeuf bourguignon and pommes purées, and sipped at a glass of Bordeaux wine. He sat next to a Minister, a dignified man in a long robe who commanded the hushed respect of the other Chadians at the table.

"Minister, is it true that President Habre went down to the cells and strangled two prisoners with his bare hands?" said Geldof.

The remark came out of the blue and the Minister looked puzzled. "What is this 'strangled'?" he asked.

"You know, strangled him," said Geldof. "Like this." Geldof twisted round in his chair, seized the Minister by the throat and shook him to and fro. The other Chadian officials watched in awe. There are people serving long sentences in jails in N'Djamena for far less heinous offences than assaulting a Minister in a restaurant.

The Minister took it very well. He straightened his robe and smoothed back his hair. "Yes, Mr Geldof, I understand very clearly what you mean by strangling. I have not heard that story."

The President of Chad is not, understandably for the leader of such a tortured country, a relaxed man. On the day after the dinner with the Ministers, he strode into the small audience chamber of his palace and sat, stiff and dignified, on the sofa next to Geldof. He has fine features, and slim, delicate hands. It was difficult to imagine them around the neck of an enemy, or even to imagine Habre as the ruthless rebel leader he once was. He had no time for small talk and came directly to the point. He thanked Geldof for his "personal initiative". "Despite geographic, political and ideological differences you are proof that there is international solidarity," said Habre. "Chad needs a lot of help. Despite the briefness of your stay, it will enable you to see a little of the problems that face us. We will do our best to see that the money you give us will be used properly. I hope that you will come back to Chad to see how it is used."

"Is the famine over, as some of the reports say?" Geldof asked.

"Regrettably not," said Habre. "We have had ten years of drought in succession and that is a lot. We have had relatively good rain this year but it will take a long time to solve the problem. Even if the rains continue to fall we really don't know what will happen. We also need to teach our people new methods of irrigation, we need to bring them a new system of education. They are obliged to end their old systems of agriculture, to settle and cultivate."

It was not only the afflictions of nature that weighed on Habre's mind, but also man-made disasters. For Habre they were evidently caused mainly by one man, Colonel Gadaffi of Libya. "The problems of Chad are not only drought and famine," said Habre. "There is another disease called Gadaffi." There was a story in that day's newspaper in N'Djamena which quoted the Libyan leader, who was visiting Moscow, as saying that he was not content with dominating only the north of Chad, he wanted to annex the south as well. What did Habre think of that? Was it just more Gadaffi rhetoric, or might the Libyan jets and armoured divisions start moving on N'Djamena? Habre took it seriously. "I have never thought Gadaffi was mad," he said. "He has an idea, an objective. He believes that he can lead a renaissance of Arab influence in this zone. He wants to be the head of an Arab empire which includes this part of Africa. He wants to be president of a united states of the sahel, which includes Chad, a natural extension of Libya in his view. He is being serious. He thinks he must annex Chad through iron and bloodshed. There are two means of dealing with Gadaffi. By arms, and by dialogue. We are ready to use both methods."

Fine words, but the reality had been spelt out to us by diplomats and officials. Habre cannot fight Gadaffi alone. He has neither the troops nor the arms, and nobody else is going to help him. The French and the Americans both made it clear that they would not, for Habre's sake, enter a battle which could lead to a full-scale war with Libya.

No leader that we met during the trip believed himself secure from the threat of coup or revolt. None however, not even Sankara in Burkina Faso who feels besieged by enemies at home and abroad, has as flimsy a grip on power as Habre. He realizes that he has few real friends. "I believe it was General de Gaulle who once said that states have interests but they don't have friends. So I am not surprised if France is following what it feels to be its own interests. Both France and the United States believe they have an interest in having relations with Libya. But Chad is abused and attacked and partly occupied. It has the right to ask everyone, everywhere for help."

This was not the right atmosphere for Geldof to ask his question about strangling. He sat politely next to Habre and asked cogent questions about Libya and foreign affairs. Towards the end of the interview he could restrain himself no longer. Morris asked Habre about the possibility of negotiations between Chad and Libya. Geldof formed his hands into a circle, as if gripping an imaginary throat, and applied pressure. Everyone but the President saw him do it and laughter erupted in the press corps. Habre looked puzzled. These British journalists have a strange sense of humour, he must have thought. They find negotiations with Libya amusing.

If there was a desperate quality to Geldof's humour it was hardly surprising. In the face of such colossal problems, the million dollars which the Band Aid committee in London had earmarked for Chad seemed almost irrelevant, a drop in the ocean of what the place desperately needed. What could they do? "We have to try to encourage hope," said Jenden afterwards. They had been to see a bridge project in the south of the country. The old bridge, which allowed the flow of relief aid, grain and medicine, to go from neighbouring Cameroon into Chad, had collapsed a year and a half before. "It was essential to supplies. For just over a million dollars we could build another one and call it the Band Aid bridge," said Jenden.

We packed our bags and, with relief, left our hot and waterless hotel rooms. Geldof disappeared. He had gone back for a last glance at the pool.

SUDAN
The aid quagmire

Our jet was at the end of the runway at N'Djamena airport, the engines building up to full thrust for take-off. Suddenly Jenden began a horrible chant. "Here we go, here we go, here we go," he shouted, swamping the roar of the jets. "Here we go, here we go, here we go." It sounded like football supporters at an Arsenal match, which is exactly where he learnt it 20 years before. Jenden, the philosophy graduate, architect and young tycoon, who started his own architecture practice in his 20s, had also once been a skin-head and, he admits, a bit of a hooligan. With this very chant Jenden and

Leaving Port Sudan for Ethiopia:
Geldof flourishes a sword presented to
him by local dignitaries.

his mates had rushed down the stands at the football stadium and descended on supporters of the rival team. Geldof, for all his good works and austere personal life, had also been, in the past, a bit of a lout. He told the story of a concert he gave at the Lyceum in London in the heady, violent days of punk and the Sex Pistols. A member of the audience, overcome by Geldof's singing, had marched onto the stage and hit him, hard, full in the face. Geldof fell over backwards, stunned. "I got even, though," said Geldof. "I caught up with him later and I beat the living shit out of him."

The mood on the plane seemed to change in direct contrast to the horrors of the places we visited. We left Chad like a busload of lads on a day trip to Brighton. The intercom burst into life. "This is your pilot," said the chief pilot, Vic Burt. "I don't know what you are all doing in the back, gentlemen, but stop it. Whoever shouts 'here we go' again will have to leave the plane, pronto, by the emergency exit. I can assure you, gentlemen, it is a long way down."

Cyril James, the engineer, began to make spoof in-flight announcements. "Hello," he would say. "This is Cyril, your engineer and hostess. We are flying very high and going very fast. I don't know quite where. One engine is on fire but it's all right because we have another one. The pilots are not at all concerned because they are both totally drunk and comatose. Thank you for flying British Aerospace. We look forward to having you on another flight. If there is one. Thank you, over and out."

It was fun in the back as we soared up to

35,000 feet, but in the cockpit both Burt and the co-pilot, Alan Smelt, had, potentially, a real problem. Flying in war-torn Chad is dangerous. The government, Libyan and rebel armies beneath us all had sophisticated ground-to-air missiles, and so did the rebels in southern Sudan which we were approaching fast. Our little jet, sleek and innocent on the ground, looked distinctly sinister on a radar screen. It had almost exactly the same electronic profile as a Russian MiG fighter. The pilots extinguished their navigation lights and asked us to pull down the shades on the windows. They were alert for the trail of a Sam 7 missile.

For the first time on this trip Geldof and Jenden were not cramming facts on the plane like schoolboys on the eve of an exam. Both Geldof and Jenden knew Sudan quite well. Jenden had been there frequently and Geldof had visited nine months before. He had wandered through the refugee camps in Omdurman on the edge of Khartoum where people starved to death only a few hundred yards from a huge cattle market. In the east he had been to a camp called Tukkelbab, near Kassala. It was the most desolate place he had ever seen. Thousands lived in the desert without tents, blankets, food or medicine. Families lived under the meagre protection of thorn bushes. He went there in February, one of the coolest months of the year. The temperature had been more than 100 degrees F. At night it fell to the low 40s. People caught pneumonia and died. There was cholera, measles, and diarrhoea. Geldof was shown a single sack of grain, the

camp's ration for the next week. A woman had dragged him over to a tent where her relatives were sewing a small boy into a sack. He had died that morning. The family carried him off into the desert for burial. Scenes like that had kept Geldof's outrage seething throughout the year. Band Aid had been working in Sudan since March 1985. It had spent more than $10 million on food, medical relief and transport. It avoids, on principle, setting up its own organization and seeks to work through governments and the major aid agencies, one of its objects being to channel all its money into aid, direct, and not into a costly bureaucracy to run it. In Sudan, though, this had proved impossible.

As Jenden said: "The aid organizations couldn't get their act together and reach consensus on what to do with the Band Aid millions. So either we kept making trips there, or we sent in our own bloke." They had done the latter three months before. The bloke was an English gentleman farmer in his 50s called John James, who had retired from his multi-million-pound agricultural business and volunteered to work for Band Aid in Sudan.

James was there to greet us. He looked terrible. Other agencies had a dozen people, sometimes on high salaries, running their administration. James was alone and unpaid. He got little sleep and looked dazed with fatigue. The mood of Khartoum was ominous. The airport terminal was closed. It was empty and eerie. James explained that there was a curfew, from 11

THE POLITICS OF FAMINE

International aid to Africa is not given simply out of the goodness of the donor country's heart. More often than not there are strings attached.

In the early days of aid the donors, with their memories of colonial responsibilities still fresh, were prepared to make a number of "soft" loans with low interest, and sometimes even interest-free loans, over long periods of time. But with the world economic recession the net transfer of money from the rich world to Africa slumped by 50 per cent between 1980 and 1983, and soft loans came gradually to be replaced, as the African nations were forced to renegotiate their debts, with "hard" loans based on strictly commercial rates of interest.

TIED AID

With the change came an increasing tendency to tie aid to trade agreements. In 1980 only ten per cent of bilateral aid from Britain was conditional on its being spent on British goods and services. Only two years later, in a bid to boost UK exports, that figure had risen to 25 per cent. And Canada demands that at least 80 per cent of its bilateral aid to Africa be spent with Canadian firms.

The unfortunate side-effect of this is that it ties many aid projects to Western technology, which the last ten years have shown to be of only limited use in Africa.

Today the continent is a white elephant's graveyard for the giant development projects of the 60s and 70s. World Bank high-technology agricultural projects lie abandoned in southern Ethiopia. Massive hydro-electric dams in eastern Sudan have silted up for lack of maintenance. A vast rice project in Mali is producing only ten per cent of the crop intended because of changes in the flow of the river. A 240-hectare plantation of drip-fed eucalyptus in Niger has produced 264,000 trees but at a cost so high the experiment will never be repeated.

But despite this, aid investment in the small-scale local initiatives which might produce better results remains low. Latest figures show that rain-fed agriculture, which provides 95 per cent of the Sahel's cereals, had received only 4.5 per cent of recent aid, while 28 per cent went on cash crops. A meagre 1.5 per cent went on anti-soil-erosion and water-harvesting projects—such projects do not produce the same kickbacks to Western industry as the old-style projects do. Britain, meanwhile, is still committed to projects like its £75 million contribution towards a huge power station for the capital of Sudan.

REPRESSIVE REGIME

But often aid has not only trade but also directly political considerations attached to it. The repressive nature of its Marxist regime and its military links with the Soviet Union mean that, though Ethiopia receives large amounts of relief aid from the West, its level of development aid, for the long-term work which would prevent the next famine, is one of the lowest per capita for any developing country in the world. The United States, in particular, though it is pledged to donate one third of Ethiopia's total food needs in 1986, strictly controls its donations to the extent that its grain can only be used for eating (relief) not planting (development). And by donating that aid through American charities it is quite knowingly undermining the Ethiopian Government's Relief and Rehabilitation Commission, which even the regime's opponents concede is the best indigenous relief organization in Africa. Conversely in Sudan, which is militarily and strategically sympathetic to the USA and which has no effective official relief body, the Americans ploughed almost one million tons of grain into the world's biggest ever relief operation, not through a network of agencies as in Ethiopia, but using a commercial trucking company. The plan was to show socialist Ethiopia how much better private enterprise could cope with famine. Unfortunately it was not a resounding success: the US Agency for International Development underestimated the difficulty of the terrain, the paralyzing bureaucracy of the Sudanese Government, the corruption and inefficiency of Sudan Railways and the contribution which could have been made by the various agencies and charities whose offers of help with transport were turned down.

Fear of political repercussions can lead to problems too. In 1984–85 the United Nations High Commission for Refugees in Sudan was aware of the large numbers of Ethiopian refugees fleeing from war and famine in Eritrea and Tigre, but was unable to step up camps in anticipation of their arrival for fear of being accused of having lured the people into Sudan.

The African countries themselves get tied up in the politics of famine too. The Ethiopian Government's controversial resettlement scheme is seen by many as a crude attempt to rob the rebels of all their supporters.

CUTS IN AID

Even domestic politics can affect aid, as is clear in Britain from the Conservative Party's commitment to cutting public spending. Over the past six years, under the leadership of Mrs Thatcher, Britain's aid budget has been cut in real terms (after allowing for inflation) by about 17 per cent. In 1979 Britain gave more aid (as a percentage of its gross national product) than any other of the world's seven leading industrialized nations. But by 1984 the British contribution had fallen from 0.52 per cent of GNP to 0.33 per cent (compared with a UN target of 0.7 per cent). Now Britain is third from bottom, with Italy expected to overtake her this year. Most of the money given to Ethiopia and Sudan in the past 12 months was simply diverted from funds already earmarked for other third-world countries.

---

pm to 5 am. There had been an attempted and easily aborted coup against the Government a few weeks before. Most of the army officers behind it had been caught, but government troops were mopping up those who remained. They were weeding out the arms caches from Khartoum at night.

James gave us our first pieces of official paper, curfew passes. Our pockets would soon be crammed with others. Sudanese bureaucracy is notorious, and took up endless, pointless hours of James's time. We needed passes to take photographs and film, passes to leave Khartoum, passes to return, a different pass, from a different ministry, for every place we visited. These were not mere formalities. An ITN tele-vision crew had been arrested in Port Sudan the day before. They had passes to go to Port Sudan, passes to return, passes to film. They did not have the special pass for filming inside the port. The police pounced and they were thrown in jail.

We drove, with extreme caution, through the deserted streets to the Grand Hotel, a seedy and depressing place, on the south bank of the Blue Nile. Geldof perked up when he saw his room. He had the presidential suite, a pink and purple extravaganza which had been vacated that morning by the Chairman of the PLO, Yasser Arafat, who had been in Khartoum on one of his flying visits.

In the morning Geldof and Jenden went to the hospital, as patients. Geldof emer-

Right top The ride into Addis Ababa, capital of Ethiopia. *Right below* Geldof and Jenden flank Berhane Deressa, deputy head of the Ethiopian Government Relief and Rehabilitation Commission at a press conference in Addis Ababa. The board behind shows a breakdown of the past year's donations from the world. *Overleaf* Bole airport, Addis Ababa. Taking grain from the airport store to the waiting Hercules.

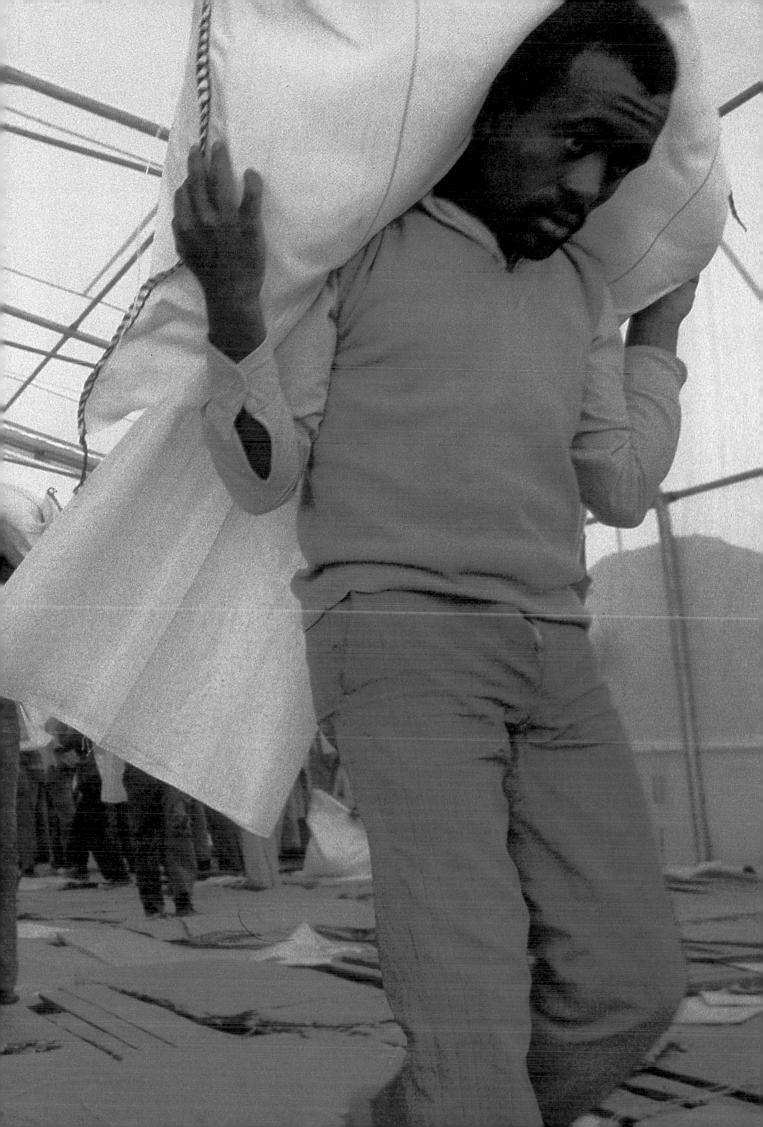

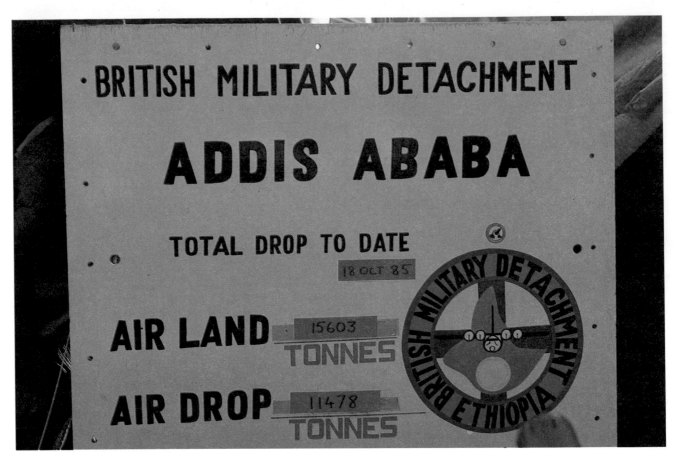

BRITISH MILITARY DETACHMENT

ADDIS ABABA

TOTAL DROP TO DATE

18 OCT 85

AIR LAND   15603
TONNES

AIR DROP   11478
TONNES

BRITISH MILITARY DETACHMENT ETHIOPIA

Above **Sign outside the emergency aid ops room, Bole airport, Addis Ababa.** *Right* **Geldof straps in for the helicopter flight across the Ethiopian highlands.**

ged with a huge bandage, like a miniature turban, on his big toe. Jenden's trousers were soaked in blood. The surgeon had excised a huge abcess from his leg. Like survivors of a battle they limped together into the Hilton Hotel for the big meeting of the trip. The conference room was packed. More than 60 different relief agencies work in Sudan and all of them had sent representatives. Band Aid intended to disperse a large slice of its money in Sudan, and the agencies wanted a piece of the action.

Geldof's voice could be heard from the lobby of the Hilton as he went through what had become a ritual speech on this trip. He wanted the agencies to reach consensus on what should be spent where. He didn't know; they should tell him. He could give some money to each of them but that, as Geldof graphically put it, would be like throwing shit and hoping some stuck. The major problem in Sudan, some of the agencies pointed out, was the lack of infrastructure or proper government control. The bureaucracy was in chaos.

The government bodies responsible for famine and refugees had only the haziest idea of the situation in the country and no accurate statistics. Nobody knew how many had died in the famine in 1985. It could have been a few hundred thousand, or as many as a million people. There were no accurate figures for the numbers of people affected by famine at the time we arrived. There were absurd anomalies. James told Geldof that there was a surplus of grain in the east, where merchants grew rich from hoarding cereals, and a deficit in

the west. The Government could not afford to buy the surplus. When the agencies tried to do so the merchants inflated the price. It was cheaper to import food aid. There were frequent strikes by lorry drivers who were bargaining with the agencies for more money, and this seriously delayed the transportation of grain. Fuel was almost impossible to buy, even at inflated black-market prices. In Port Sudan there were lorries queuing for two days at petrol stations.

In the lobby some disaffected members of major agencies sought out the international press. It quickly became clear that Band Aid was not popular among the agencies in Sudan. There were a number of serious criticisms. The head of one of the largest agencies, who asked that his identity should not be disclosed, said that he was sick of Geldof and Band Aid.

His main point was that Band Aid had arrived "thinking the rest of us were a crowd of idiots, that they could succeed where we had failed".

"It was an arrogant attitude," he said. "And now they have made mistakes." They had gone into the transport business with a fleet of more than 70 lorries, 16 British staff and 130 locals. It was, he said, too little too late. The lorries had been needed six months earlier, before the rains came and made the roads impassable.

He was joined by a London representative of another major agency, who also asked that his name not be published. Geldof would say later: "Why can't they say this in the open meeting? I was just across the lobby in the conference room.

But they wouldn't come out with it." It was a valid point. The two critics said they did not want to cause public embarrassment. Their behaviour symbolized, however, the rivalry and backstabbing which has made Sudan a viper's nest for the aid agencies.

The critics said that Band Aid talked too much and did too little. Why were they sitting in the conference room of the Hilton Hotel when they could have given the money away to the existing charities by bankers' order, from London? Some agencies like Save the Children were running out of money. The United Nations High Commission for Refugees was curtailing its programme in the east for lack of funds. "It is criminal that they are not giving this money to the groups who are already here," said one of them. "People who are good at raising money are usually not good at spending it. They are wasting everyone's time. Band Aid does not need its academics and experts vetting projects back in London. All the major agencies have their own vetting procedures, done by people in the field. Band Aid is merely duplicating what has been done," he said.

"Band Aid should be brave enough to take the risk and give money where it is needed, to Oxfam or Save the Children. They are being holier than thou about how they spend their money. And I'm not sure they realize how agencies really work. When emergencies happen they spend

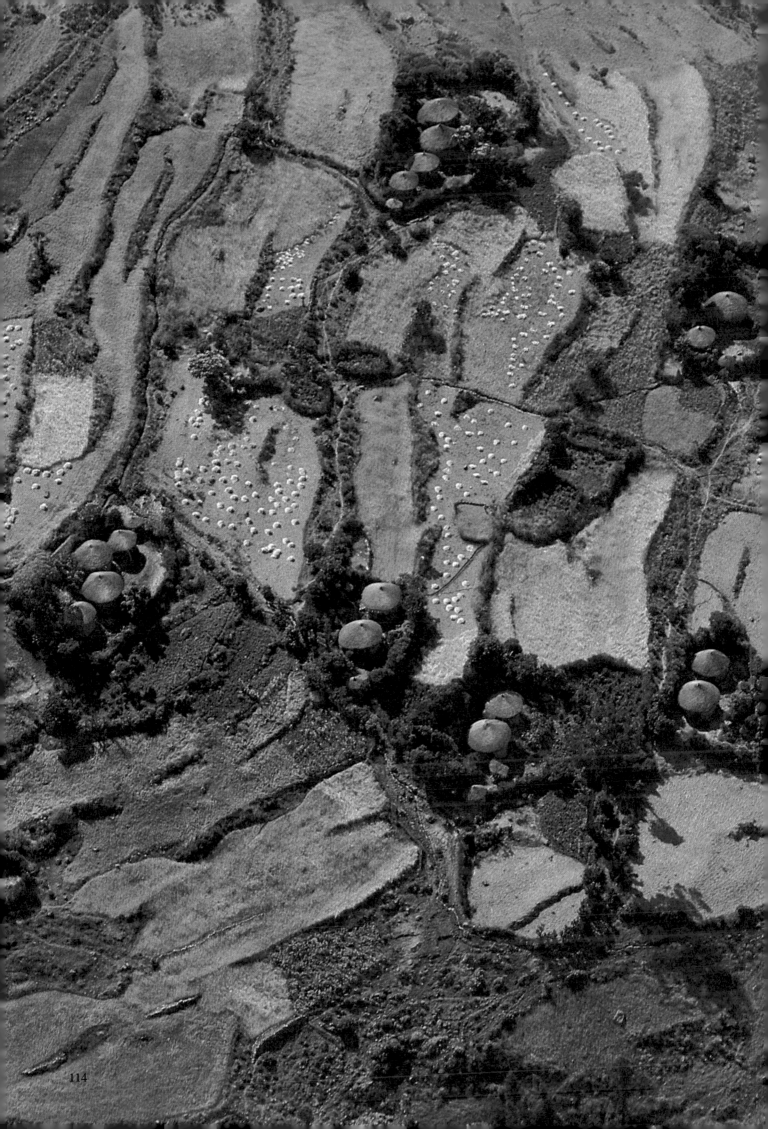

money first, then fund-raise to pay the bills. Band Aid money should have gone to pay for projects that have already been completed but not paid for."

Geldof and Jenden took the criticism well. Band Aid was in good shape in Sudan and both felt confident. Geldof pointed out that no agency, however big, has come out of Sudan smelling of roses. They hoped to come out smelling better than most. Their trucks were now running, after initial problems, from Port Sudan at the most competitive rate in the country. Band Aid let any agency use the 70 lorries. They charged cost, about £40 a ton, to move goods from Port Sudan to Khartoum. The commercial rate charged by Sudanese companies was £120. They had been asked to go into transport by the United Nations. They had done so and it had worked.

"The facts belie the criticisms," said Geldof. "It makes no sense to say we should have bought the trucks six months ago. Six months ago we didn't have the money; it was before the Live Aid concerts. Nor is it fair to compare us to an ordinary agency. We have deliberately not set up our own general operations structure. Instead we have given money or transport facilities to 23 agencies here. Not all agency projects work and we have to make sure that any projects funded by Band Aid can and do work. It is our responsibility to ensure that the money, 100 per cent of it, goes, without the administrative costs that most agencies pay, direct to the people that need it. That's our job. That's why it has worked. Aid agencies are answerable to us for how they spend Band Aid money because we hold it in trust for the people who gave it. Having said that, the agencies do brilliant work and they are manned by experts. That's why Band Aid has never attempted to duplicate their function, but merely to fund them and their activities. Unfortunately, not all the agencies have got worthwhile projects, and we have limited funds. Also, we can't just give it to the big ones; there are other smaller agencies with equally important projects."

"We try to fund projects that can't get money from the big donors," said Jenden. "We have to look around and see which ones are worthwhile."

Despite the reservations of the agencies, the Sudanese Government liked Band Aid, and the President, General Swareddahab, wanted to give Geldof a medal. We assembled in the reception room of the palace in Khartoum, a few yards from the plaque which marks the spot where the British military commander, General Gordon, was killed by the Mahdi a century ago. The chief of protocol at the palace went

After the rains: a village on the fertile plateau just north of Addis Ababa. Heaps of straw from the early harvest dot the fields. *Overleaf* The entire population of Ganamba, an isolated village in the Ethiopian highlands, waves to Geldof's helicopter.

straight to the only person among us wearing a tie.

"Mr Geldof," he said. "We wish to welcome you to Khartoum, and the President will present you with an honour."

"I am not Mr Geldof," said Vallely of *The Times*. "He is over there."

The chief of protocol looked nervously at the ruffled Geldof, who was dressed in his best, with a pink shirt, baggy blue trousers and sneakers.

Swareddahab was smiling and relaxed for a man facing coups, civil war, famine, drought and bankruptcy. He awarded Geldof the Order of the Two Niles (Second Class), an impressive blue and gold medal made by Spinks of London. What, Geldof wondered later, did the Order of the Two Niles (First Class) look like, and what did you have to do to get it?

They sat together on the sofa. Geldof did what he does well—asking the blunt questions that other people do not dare, or get the opportunity, to ask the presidents of distant countries.

"Could you do us a favour?" said Geldof.

"Yes, what is it, Bob?" said the President.

"Have a word with Libya for us, General. Would you ask your new friend Colonel Gadaffi what he's doing about the famine victims and the displaced people in northern Chad. Hissein Habre says that they live in a ghetto up there, without any sort of food or medical relief."

"I will certainly raise that with the Libyans," said the President.

Geldof also raised a matter closer to home, the grain surpluses in eastern Sudan that weren't reaching the people in the west. What was the President going to do about it? The President was not sure. "The Government does not have the money to buy the surplus," he said.

"It's a mess," said Geldof.

"Yes, it's a real mess," said the President.

Sudan is the biggest country in the continent and it is sadly appropriate that its mess is a microcosm of the mess of all Africa. Less than ten years ago its President was predicting that Sudan would soon become "the breadbasket of Africa". By 1985 it had become the scene of the largest famine relief operation in the history of the world. If ever there was proof that famine is an act of man rather than an act of God it is there in Sudan.

The Government of President Jafaar Nimeiry, which was overthrown in a coup in April 1985 as a result of popular dissatisfaction which derived in part from

Ganamba villagers amid the stubble of a successful barley harvest. The seeds had been flown in by helicopter three months before. *Overleaf* A formal welcome for Geldof from the villagers at the gates of the monastery at Ganamba.

his handling of the famine crisis, knew that there were serious problems in Darfour in the west of Sudan three years ago. The provincial governor sent in constant reports about the deteriorating situation but they were ignored. At the time, Nimeiry was hoping for massive agricultural investment from the oil-rich Arab states to turn the plains of Sudan into cash-producing wheatlands on the scale of those in Canada; his hopes would have been scuppered by any suggestion that there was famine on the extremities of the land. Indeed, towards the end of that time Nimeiry had actually gone on record as attributing the famine in Ethiopia to divine retribution on a nation which had turned its back on Allah. As he had just announced himself as a born-again Muslim and reintroduced the harsh Sharia law, with its public floggings, amputations and executions, an appeal for famine relief would have been politically embarrassing.

So the provincial governor went unheard and, in the end, resigned in frustration. Bodies like Oxfam, Save the Children and the World Food Programme were the next to warn Nimeiry of the scale of the problem, but he ignored them too. It was not until the United States Agency for International Development (USAID) began to put on the pressure that Nimeiry acknowledged the famine and made an international appeal for aid. Such is the inverted sense of priorities of most African governments: peasants starving in the countryside are an irrelevance; workers rioting in the town are a consideration; but the influence of Washington or Moscow is decisive.

Jafaar Nimeiry's culpability did not end there. The inheritance which African countries had been left by the colonizing powers was a mixed one. On the bad side, the 19th-century scramble for Africa had resulted in the map of the continent being decided by the dictates of the straight line; the boundaries marked spheres of influence for the different European powers which took little account of the area's indigenous nationalities and concentrated largely on dividing the exploitable resources. The result was that the colonies to which Europe later gave independence were not really countries as we understand them. Sudan was an arbitrary amalgam of Arab Muslims in the north with black Christians and animists in the south, who shared little. Even these groups were divided and sub-divided. There may not be quite so many in Sudan as in neighbouring Chad—where there are no less than 250 different languages and racial sub-groups—but almost. Darfour, though it is in Sudan, lies so far to the west that it finds itself halfway between the Atlantic Ocean and the Red Sea, and local people regard Khartoum as a foreign capital and speak of "going to Sudan".

On the good side, the British left Sudan with one of the best railway systems in Africa. Yet in the 30 years since independence—more than half of them under

Above **A parting gift from the monks of Ganamba.** *Right* **Headman, Ganamba village.** *Overleaf* **Women of Ganamba, their tukuls (straw-roofed huts) in the background.**

Nimeiry—there was little maintenance and no real investment in the railway. This was partly an attempt to undermine the strength of the railway workers' union, the most powerful trade union in Sudan and an implacable opponent of Nimeiry. It was also to give scope for the build-up of a private enterprise system of road transport which would win the support of the entrepreneurial classes which were not Nimeiry's natural supporters. Nimeiry's neglect of the railway system, which subsequently became one of the most corrupt and inefficient bodies in Africa, was to

prove a crucial element in the failure of the famine relief effort.

Nimeiry's attitude to the railways was symptomatic of a greater evil.

The week before he was deposed, the President of Sudan telephoned the manager of the Khartoum football club El Hilal and told him to sack the team's

Brazilian coach. The manager was surprised. In the past the President had always been a supporter of the capital's other main team, El Mirriekh—and not just a supporter who cheered from the grandstand but one who conferred all sorts of concessions and privileges on his favourite club. Why the sudden interest in the rival team?

"Foreign coaches are bad for Sudanese football," the President had said. "That is why footballers in the Sudan are not good. All foreign coaches must be sacked."

El Hilal's Signor Naguerra packed his bags. The coach-in-chief of all Sudanese football clubs from then on would be Jafaar Nimeiry.

Trivial as it was, the incident was typical of the way Nimeiry's increasing megalomania led him to intervene personally in the most minute decisions about the way his country was run. Under Nimeiry, junior civil servants often took orders direct from the President; bank managers had phone calls from him instructing them on the movement of cash from one account to another; judges were promoted and downgraded to fit Nimeiry's political whim of the moment; the security police was filled with gangsters. Nimeiry not only corrupted institutions he had inherited from the British in 1956, destroying the independence of the machinery of government, of the judiciary and the police; he also systematically destroyed any figure of respectable opposition who could have provided the reminder of a political alternative.

Worst of all, Nimeiry revived the civil war in the south. Through an arrogant and provocative act of regional reorganization he put an end to four years of peace which, though it was uneasy, had been sufficient to allow the vital development of the natural resources on which the future prosperity of the entire nation depends. The untapped oil reserve there is estimated to be the largest in Africa and the half-completed Jongelei canal could add to the flow of the Nile billions of gallons of vital water currently lost in the swamps of the Sudd. The war is currently costing $1 million a day.

It was in this context that the drought of the past decade turned in 1985 to widespread famine. The Government of the United States decided upon a swift and unilateral response, partly out of humanitarian concern but partly because the maintenance of a friendly government in Sudan is a cornerstone of America's foreign policy in the area, which lies strategically between the Soviet-dominated Horn of Africa and the instability of the Middle East. It decided to boost its food aid from 319,039 tons to almost a million tons. It would cost nearly $400 million and be the biggest free food programme ever. The plan was to get the food to the areas of greatest need and stockpile it there before the rains came and made the roads impassable.

It was a bold and generous plan but politics, ideology and the sheer geography of the Sudan doomed it to failure.

The greed and personal ambition of the country's politicians and bureaucrats had robbed it of the infrastructure of railways, roads and efficient services indispensable to such a massive operation. The railways, as was entirely predictable, consistently failed to move the quantities of grain required. And aid workers also found themselves up against the corrupting Arabic ethic of laissez-faire mercantilism and the Sudanese people's lack of nationhood and sense of the common good. "It is impossible to motivate workers loading food in Khartoum or at the halfway point at Kosti with any sense that it is their brothers who are dying in Darfour," said one Western aid worker. "They are very charitable when it comes to giving alms to the poor around them, but those over the hill? Forget it."

Reaganite ideology insisted that the logistics of the entire famine relief effort be placed in the hands of a single American-Sudanese commercial firm to prove to socialist Ethiopia next door just how much better private enterprise could do these things. The result was a stubborn refusal by USAID to allow charities, including Band Aid, Save the Children and the Red Cross, to join in with the transportation of food until it was too late. Even the United Nations was initially excluded with the argument that the price of hiring trucks would be artificially inflated by the entry of any second agency onto the market.

The vast geographical problems of Sudan added the final handicap. The relief lorries had to travel over 800 miles of roadless sand, carrying all their fuel and spares with them.

"You try taking your car to the beach and driving it for 800 yards," says Geldof. He is speaking from personal experience. The Band Aid party flew out to northern Darfour and then travelled in landrovers from El Geneina to famine-hit districts. Geldof's own vehicle got stuck in the fine sand and, after being dug out, passed food lorries even more firmly entrenched, with the treacherous sand nearly covering the wheels.

"And the rains are over now!" exclàimed Geldof in disbelief as the labourers who rode with one of the lorries began unloading the 30 tons of food it carried. They were going to empty the entire truck, dig it out, and then load it again. The whole tiresome procedure might have to be repeated only a few hundred yards on.

"During the rains this sand turns into mud which is like glue. Now the trucks can move slowly; then they could not move at all," said Ekber Menemencioglu, a diminutive moustachioed Turk from the UN's High Commission for Refugees (UNHCR), who had spent the previous six months in a continual battle against the climate and terrain of these desert wastes.

This, he told us, was the food still struggling through in October which should have been in place in June. Hundreds of thousands of people had died as a result.

"Even more would have died had it not been for these," said Ekber, pointing to the wiry little bushes which dotted the flat sands. "They are called 'mokheit'. At the height of the dry season they produce a berry. It is poisonous but if it is steeped in water for 15 days and then boiled for seven hours it can be eaten. This is what kept thousands alive when all the technology of the West could not," he fulminated. In Ekber, Geldof had finally met his match for righteous indignation. The little Turk exploded volcanically and often, only later turning to the journalists to say: "You'd better not quote me on that."

"He's great," said Geldof with admiration. "After all this time out here his sense of outrage is still intact."

With good cause. Things in the west of Sudan have, at last, improved. Geldof saw food and Help the Aged blankets arriving and an impressive Oxfam water-purification scheme at a camp for Chadian refugees at Azernay, all of which Band Aid had a hand in funding. But the old problems were there still, just below the surface.

"It was terrifying," says Geldof. At one point when he opened the door of his vehicle a German army ration biscuit fell out. There was quite literally a riot. There were about 300 people milling around. They all dived for the biscuit. Behind them there must have been a thousand people. They could not have known what the rush was for, but they knew it was for something, so they rushed too. They all piled in. A woman carrying two babies, one to each breast, was crushed beneath them. Then the camp guards came in with whips flailing.

"All over one f . . . ing biscuit. This is the world we live in."

Later in the week Geldof visited a second camp, this time on the eastern extremity of Sudan, by the border with Ethiopia. There the problem was different. The physical situation was under control but the question remained: how, now, do you avoid people becoming dependent upon free food and the services of camp life?

It was a half-hour drive from the airstrip at Kassala to the sprawling conglomeration of mat dwellings and tents which is now said to be the third largest city in Sudan. Its name is Wad Sherifay and it is to be found, deliberately hidden from the eyes of the native Sudanese, behind a cluster of huge grotesque rocks which look like the knuckles of some giant fist.

Driving through the camp towards the office at its centre, Geldof spotted vivid pink flowers, the product of assiduous watering and jealous protection, growing in the bare dust outside one of Wad Sherifay's half dozen clinics. Substantial dirt roads had been worn between the rows of shelters and tents. Their inmates somehow had found the wherewithal to acquire a little livestock; donkeys wandered the camp's crowded square mile and the odd goat could be seen grubbing in the dust.

Sudan's largest refugee camp, Geldof discovered, is taking on a disconcerting atmosphere of permanence. What was once an emergency refuge has become a food aid shanty town which UN officials are concerned may be there for another ten or 12 years.

Its inhabitants, smiling and well-fed, queued for their rations in distribution centres which were as well-organized as Western supermarkets. Each had four check-outs, complete with a maze of wooden barriers to shepherd the Ethiopian refugees every ten days through a series of pick-up points to collect their five kilos of cereal, 600 grams of black beans, 600 mls of oil, cake of soap, and, on every third visit, a ration of salt and sugar. The supplies stood on stout wooden pallets in large piles which are regularly replenished from the camp's central stores. At the time of Band Aid's visit Wad Sherifay was consuming 800 tons of food every day.

The clinics were quiet and efficient too. Malnutrition rates, which stood at 50 per cent when Geldof was last here in February, were, even including new arrivals, down to 20 per cent. There was flesh on the biceps and thighs of the adults and children. The stench so characteristic of these places, a sickly-sweet miasmic odour of sweat, faeces and decay, had disappeared almost entirely. The death rate, once more than 120 a day, was now lower than that of a modern European city of comparable size.

In the camp hospital the medical stores were full of drugs, including anti-cholera supplies paid for by Band Aid. "This has been one of the great success stories of the famine, which is probably why you never hear about it from the newspapers or the television. Problems with cholera were anticipated so when the outbreak came the camps contained the death rate to only two or three per cent. In the towns and villages outside it was more than ten per cent. Our success would not have been possible without the foresight of people like Band Aid who had the drugs here, ready and waiting," one doctor told Geldof.

There were still difficulties, but they were not overwhelming, he said. The sense of relief infected Geldof too, who for once actually paused briefly on his tour of the wards to play with a doll with a little two-year-old being treated for TB. He said nothing, but she was the same age as his own daughter, Fifi.

"It's easy to forget amidst all the horror that these are still children who need toys to play with," he said afterwards in a kind of apology. Throughout the trip he had been avoiding situations like that. Geldof is only too aware that these are the occasions the photographers watch for and he is sensitive to the fact that these

situations produce the kind of picture he most dislikes—the white man patronizing the little native child, not that anyone present at the time would doubt the sincerity of Geldof's compassion.

But if things are looking better in Wad Sherifay it simply poses a new problem: "What do we do with these people now," as Jim Carl of the UN's Development Programme put it in Khartoum. "Most of them are refugees from war rather than famine. They cannot go home because the fighting continues, indeed at the moment it is getting worse. But because they want to return eventually to their homes in Eritrea they cannot be permanently resettled elsewhere in Sudan. There is no seasonal labour here for them; there is not even enough of that for the native Sudanese. And the land at Wad Sherifay is so poor that they cannot farm it. What is the alternative to carrying on feeding them until the war is over? So far it has been going for 23 years. These people may be with us here for another ten or twelve."

Some attempts had been made to reduce the size of the huge camp. There were regular plans to ferry refugees to other camps, like the one they called Fau Five (there are four others there already) which was created for the purpose. But the shipment of refugees from one part of the country to another causes internal political problems for the Sudanese. At the time of Geldof's visit Fau Five was still empty and the Swiss Disaster Team which had been waiting there since the spring was threatening to leave. A further complication is that the Eritreans themselves prefer life at Wad Sherifay within sight of the hills of their homeland. Whenever attempts have been made to move them in the past, thousands have disappeared overnight into the hills, the surrounding villages, or the town of Kassala itself, only to return a few days later.

People come and go with such regularity that the number officially registered in the camp is now always out of touch with reality. Sudanese Government officials gave Geldof the figure of 185,000 people; aid workers said it was 130,000.

The numbers had been swollen in recent months by an extra 50,000 people fleeing from the increased fighting in Eritrea. More than 15,000 arrived in the days after the rebel-held town of Barentu fell to the Ethiopian army in August and the Government's Koonamah militia began bayonetting civilians in reprisal executions, according to Wad Sherifay's Sudanese administrator, Mohammed Osman.

When Geldof had first come across him eight months before, he was happily talking about the imminent closure of the place and his return to his real job as a development agronomist. Now that event seemed further away than ever.

"All we can do in a place like this is hope to alleviate the suffering a little," said Geldof. "The real problem here is the war and that is something over which no aid agency can have any control."

That much was clear when Band Aid's jet left Sudan for the last country of the trip, Ethiopia. We were flying at 30,000 feet when we crossed the border—which, as it turned out, was just as well. Shortly afterwards tracer bullets came sparkling up like a November firework towards the plane. Below and, thanks to the foresight of the pilots, well out of range, the war between the Ethiopian army and the Eritrean rebels was continuing. Geldof had entered the most difficult phase of his African journey.

ETHIOPIA
Ideology and holocaust

Geldof loped across the VIP lounge at Addis airport and hugged a thickset man with a moustache. He was Berhane Deressa, deputy commissioner of the Ethiopian Relief and Rehabilitation Commission (RRC) and a big shot in the Ethiopian political hierarchy. Deressa hugged him back. There was a lot of back slapping and shaking of hands. Few Western visitors, even members of foreign aid agencies bringing far larger cheques than Band Aid's for famine relief, get this kind of welcome from the Marxist-Leninist Government of Ethiopia. Relations between aid agencies and the Government are polite at best, normally tense and often downright hostile.

"Bob, I've got your programme for you," said Deressa.

"So you're trying to programme me already are you, you Marxist bastard," said Geldof.

"You running dog of imperialism, you capitalist swine," said Deressa.

"Politburo ponce," said Geldof.

There was more laughing and slapping of backs.

Geldof, it quickly became apparent, has an easy relationship with officials and functionaries of the Workers' Party of Ethiopia. And that has meant more than just a hug and a slap on the back at Addis airport. Band Aid has operated in Ethiopia with an official sanction that other agencies envy. It is difficult to see quite why.

The explanation perhaps lies in Geldof's personality and Band Aid itself. As Geldof had said on the plane: "Band Aid is something to everyone. For the right it represents self-help. For the left it shows the power of the ordinary people." Geldof, for all his moral and political rhetoric, is not an ideologue and would not fit well into any known political party. That evening, over dinner in an Addis restaurant, he lambasted a senior Workers' Party member about "all this Marxist crap" as keenly as he had laid into the French Minister in Mali and as he would, on his return to Europe, slag off the EEC parliamentarians in Strasbourg.

We arrived in Addis 12 hours before

schedule. Deressa and the immigration and security officials had been dragged from their homes. A diplomat from the British embassy had had to leave an official function and arrived at the airport looking disgruntled. We also had a problem in the shape of Vallely of *The Times*. Vallely had been to Ethiopia before and had written articles critical of the Ethiopian Government's handling of the famine crisis. There were officials waiting at the very steps of the aircraft for him.

The Government does not like criticism. It censors any hint of it in its own newspapers, and foreign journalists who knock the system are not allowed back. In London, before we left, the Ethiopian embassy had pointedly refrained from putting a visa into Vallely's passport. He had wondered whether to go with Geldof on this last leg of the journey. Geldof had advised him "to busk it": to arrive and see what happened.

The security men looked through our passports, looked at Vallely, then took him away to a room at the airport. There they told him: "You are not welcome here. You hate Ethiopia. You hate Ethiopians. You will stay at the airport. You will not leave this room until you get on the first plane in the morning."

Geldof, who on the first day of our trip had expressed the passionate belief that the press was scum (something the Ethiopian Government would heartily agree with), now became its champion. "I don't want to cause any trouble," he told the officials. "And I must stress that I am not threatening to pull any of Band Aid's money out of Ethiopia. But he has been on the trip with us through Africa and that's how it's going to stay. If he goes in the morning, then so do I and I won't come back. This is not an idle threat. We have our own plane and we will all leave on it in the morning."

He gave them a lecture on the freedom of the press. "I'm only here," he said, "because I've read the kind of things Vallely and other journalists have written about Ethiopia. You have to allow them to say what they like. Even if they sometimes tell lies you have to allow them the freedom to do it."

The officials retired in confusion. There was, it emerged later, a battle between the internal security people who keenly desired to chuck Vallely out, and the RRC, who could see the damage their image abroad among donors and donor countries would suffer if Geldof left next morning in a blaze of publicity. The RRC won the day; Vallely stayed, as a non-person without a visa or an entry stamp, until Geldof left. It was a brisk plunge into the politics of Ethiopia, which would grow murkier during our trip.

We drove at night through the deserted streets of Addis. There has been a curfew there for so long—about 15 years—that people have forgotten quite why. The civil wars that Ethiopia is fighting in the provinces of Eritrea, Tigre and Wollo, and

in the south, do not impinge on the capital. "We quite like the curfew now," said an RRC official. "It means you don't get drunk, or stay out late with women. I don't think I could afford it if they stopped it."

Addis is the only African capital which has huge posters of white men plastered over walls and dominating the central square. They are Marx, Lenin and Engels. There are revolutionary banners and slogans everywhere, and large portraits of Ethiopia's leader, Comrade Mengistu Haile-Mariam.

Mengistu is referred to by his full title in all newspaper articles and radio and television broadcasts. It takes up a large amount of space and airtime. The television news has room for little else. The title is: "Comrade Mengistu Haile-Mariam, General Secretary of the Central Committee of the Workers' Party of Ethiopia, Chairman of the Provisional Military Administrative Council and Commander in Chief of the Revolutionary Armed Forces of Socialist Ethiopia." The West, especially the Americans, hoped that the vast quantities of aid poured into

Ethiopia during the terrible famine of 1985 would lure Mengistu away from his close relationship with Russia and make him more amenable to the West. It didn't.

The 11-member politburo has two slightly pro-Western members: the Ministers of Justice and Industry. When the amount of foreign aid exploded in 1984 their influence seemed to increase. Then the politburo swung back. It is now more pro-Soviet than ever before. People the Government (which is known as the Dergue) believes suspect or ideologically impure have been detained. There was a coup attempt at the end of April 1985 by members of the army and airforce. It was ruthlessly put down. There were 90 arrests and several executions. There are Cuban troops based just outside Addis who act as a praetorian guard for Mengistu, a defence against any future rebellion in the ranks of his own armed forces.

We went to the Hilton Hotel in Addis, which is a shock. Ethiopia is one of the world's poorest countries. It has one of the finest Hilton Hotels, with a large pool, tennis courts,

Alomata, Wollo, Ethiopia. "OK, *you* take *my* picture," said Geldof, giving the child his camera. *Overleaf* The feeding centre at Alomata. These two sacks each weigh 22.5 kilos (50 lbs) and they represent a fortnight's supply for a family of six.

bars, restaurants and a nightclub. Some of the suites on the "executive floor" look straight down onto a shanty town next door where people live in corrugated-iron sheds. Sewers run down its main streets. The cost of one night in a Hilton suite is double the annual income of the majority of Ethiopian peasants.

In the morning we all felt better than we had done for two weeks. We had slept well, in the cool, thin, pure air of Addis which is almost 8000 feet above sea level on a high plateau. It is, however, difficult to breathe at this height, and people who exert themselves too much get sick. The long, winding drive up to the British embassy compound is nicknamed "cardiac hill" by the diplomats.

Geldof and Jenden had their first major meeting of the day in the offices of the RRC, where they met representatives of the 47 agencies that work in Ethiopia. The offices are impressive and so is the RRC. The walls of the room are lined with green boards covered in tiny magnetic numbers and letters showing deficits and surpluses of grain and medicine, how much aid each group has given, which airforce is dropping what food where.

The RRC is recognized as being the most effective famine relief organization in the third world. It has been at work for 11 years and has a staff of 17,000. Its early-warning system, alerting both the Ethiopian Government and the world to impending disaster, is now respected. It warned about the famine in 1984 long before it occurred, but the West chose to ignore the evidence.

The officials outlined Ethiopia's problems. It had rained in 1985, but the rains had stopped too early. Forecasts indicated that the country would produce five million tons of grain, but a further million tons of food aid would be needed in 1986 to feed more than five million people affected by famine. But, if the infrastructure of aid established during the past nine months remained and if the food pledged by the West arrived, there was no reason why, next year, millions should starve to death as they had in '84 and '85.

Although the world's donors had provided a deluge of aid for Ethiopia, for which the RRC was duly grateful, it had a complaint. Deressa said that the Government was concerned that foreign donors were putting their relief through the 47 private agencies working in Ethiopia, and not through the RRC.

There are two reasons for Western reluctance to use the RRC. First, Western governments do not want to bolster a pro-Soviet regime. Second, they do not want to become involved in the most controversial issue in Ethiopia: the politics of famine and the Government's resettlement programme.

Most diplomats and foreign aid workers speak only privately and in whispers about resettlement, for fear of offending the Government. Resettlement involves moving about one and a half million Ethiopians from the northern provinces of Wollo and

Tigre to areas many hundreds of miles away in the south and southwest.

The process began in earnest late in 1984. Some 542,000 people were moved between November 1984 and August 1985, at an estimated financial cost of $2,500 per person. The official explanation for this vast displacement is simple: the land in Wollo and Tigre has been ruined by drought, overpopulation and bad farming for years. The people cannot live on it. They either move or slowly starve to death. The Government plans to move a further 200,000 people by next June, and another half a million by the end of 1986. It wants the private agencies and Western governments to give money for the resettlement programme.

Geldof, as his behaviour during this trip has clearly shown, is not afraid to speak his mind. At the meeting that morning he held up a piece of paper. It was a copy of *The Wall Street Journal* which carried a report of an investigation carried out by a reputable American group, Cultural Survival Inc., which included on its board several Harvard professors. On the basis of 250 interviews with Ethiopian refugees, the investigation concluded that between 50,000 and 100,000 people had died as a direct result of the resettlement programme. "Is it true or not?" Geldof asked the meeting.

A Catholic priest, Father Jack Finucane, who heads the aid agency Concern, had no doubt it was untrue. "I've read it, and I don't believe it," he said. There had been problems but nothing on that scale. He had visited the areas, and his own group worked in some of them, and he had seen no sign of the horrors the report described. The audience agreed, overwhelmingly and volubly. It was dangerous, one of them said, to take the evidence of refugees from the camps in Sudan, as Cultural Survival had done. These people were against the Ethiopian Government and would naturally tell reporters and investigators anti-Government propaganda. The RRC officials nodded their heads vigorously. Quietly, one of the most senior aid officials passed a note to the English press. "Do not expect anyone to speak freely while the man with the blue suit is here," it said. The man in the blue suit was Berhane Deressa.

But one man refused to be bound by the conspiracy of silence. Michel Fiszbin, from the medical group Médecins Sans Frontières, was shocked and appalled by what he heard. He had been at a private meeting in the Hilton Hotel a month before, at which the press and government officials had not been present, when Father Finucane had said the opposite. He had said that half a million people had been displaced in the first phase of the resettlement programme in "horrible conditions". He had said that out of 77 resettled areas only two or three could be described as successful. As a result, he had said, 100,000 people had died.

It became clear to Geldof and his press entourage that something very odd was going on in Addis. During the next few days other agencies would, out of earshot of government officials, give their assessment of resettlement. They all agreed, in private, that it had been a disaster in 1985. They suspected that the motive behind the Government's programme was more political than humanitarian. Although it was true that some of the land the people were being moved from was barren, there was land in the same provinces where the people could have been resettled at far less cost in terms of both human life and financial resources.

These agencies, and many Western governments, believed that the people were being moved because the Ethiopian Government was fighting a civil war against the Tigrean People's Liberation Front in Tigre and Wollo. The point was to starve the rebels in these areas of both recruits and support.

There was a secondary motive: by moving people from their established communities and into the large new resettlements the Marxist Government was increasing its control over the peasants and furthering its policy of collectivizing the agriculture, much as Stalin had done in post-war Russia.

Agencies had strong evidence that people were not, as the Government claimed, moved voluntarily but were forced to go. Agency reports showed that sick and starving people were taken on the journey to the south, which sometimes took months. Many died on the way, in the trucks, the planes or the transit camps. It takes a massive infrastructure to move half a million people, and this simply did not exist. The transit camps lacked proper shelter, food or medical supplies. Families were broken up. A report by the International Red Cross, which had been given to the Government but not made public, showed that a massive 31 per cent of 756 families interviewed in transit camps had suffered some sort of family separation. Husbands, wives or children were lost, scattered across this vast country or left behind. The majority of these will never be reunited.

In its propaganda films and literature the Government paints an idyllic picture of life in the resettlement areas. Families are given a simple home, a garden, land to cultivate, seed, farm implements, livestock and medical care. It is sometimes true. Some resettlement areas do work well and thousands of students and young people have been sent in the past few months to prepare the new villages for the influx of people. But last year many of these areas had nothing: the huts were badly made and fell down; there was no seed, no farm implements, and virgin land which the people did not have the strength or knowledge to cultivate. Sanitation was

Right **People come from miles around on foot to collect their grain supply.**

non-existent. Tens of thousands of people died. Many of them had lived in the highlands of northern Ethiopia and suddenly found themselves in the hot climate and swamps of the south. Thousands died of malaria, a disease virtually unknown in the north. There were, last year, not enough doctors or drugs to cope with the terrible spread of disease.

Why were the agencies so unwilling to tell the truth, and why, when Geldof raised the issue, had the denials been so firm? The headquarters of the charity Concern, which Father Finucane works for, said that there was not really a contradiction between his two reports, at the Hilton in September and at the RRC headquarters in October. At the first meeting he had stressed the stark horror of what had happened, said Concern, to encourage the foreign ambassadors present to give aid to the resettlement areas. At the second meeting, when the press was present, he had given a more encouraging report, so that donors in the West would give aid to prevent the horrors of the past year occurring again. It is an honourable distinction, but it makes the truth of what is happening in Ethiopia difficult to establish. Other agencies said in Addis that if they give the facts in public they run the risk of offending the Ethiopian Government and losing its co-operation in their aid efforts, and that stories that reflect badly on the Government may dry up the contributions from the West.

Michel Fiszbin, from Médecins Sans Frontières, was the only agency official willing to talk in public. He says that the other agencies' reluctance to tell the truth is damaging. "The international community is pouring millions of dollars into this country but cannot make the correct decisions about how it should be spent."

There is evidence that the Government has acted on the agency reports, for example a Red Cross League investigation which was a damning indictment of the way resettlement was being carried out. Conditions in resettlement areas are now better, according to another League investigation carried out in October.

However, Fiszbin maintains that the horrors have not stopped. Just after Geldof left Addis to return to London the government militiamen went into Korem camp in Wollo, rounded up more than 600 people with sticks and whips and forced them "like cattle", says Fiszbin, into trucks to go to a resettlement transit camp. Fiszbin's organization has also been prevented by government officials from giving children intensive feeding care in a camp in Wollo. He says that 5000 children need such care and that hundreds are dying for the lack of it: "Our doctors find the bodies of children on the roads leading out of the camp." He also says the Government has stopped the organization giving dry rations to thousands of people. He believes the reason is that the Government is trying to force people to resettle. The Government's attitude is: resettle and we will give you food and assistance; stay where you are and we will not help you.

Fiszbin's outspokenness has led to a predictable government reaction.

Médecins Sans Frontières was threatened with expulsion.

"Médecins Sans Frontières talk the most and do the least," said Deressa. "We have shown them the door and they can go through it. I hope they do."

The moral issue facing Band Aid, other aid agencies and governments is whether to give relief money for the resettlement programme. The Red Cross and Médecins Sans Frontières have refused. "We cannot support a programme when we cannot lay down even the barest criteria: that people are not forced to go; that families are not broken up; that the transit is humane; that people get basic provisions when they arrive. We do not approve of resettlement. We cannot help to carry it out."

Other agencies disagree. Geldof takes a clear line. People in resettlement areas are suffering and they need help. "If we had been in existence during the second world war and we heard that people were dying in concentration camps, would we refuse to give them food and aid in those camps? Of course not. The same principle applies here. I may not agree with resettlement, but the Government is going to go ahead with it whether we agree or not. People are in need and we are here to help save lives. If we can do that in resettlement areas then so be it."

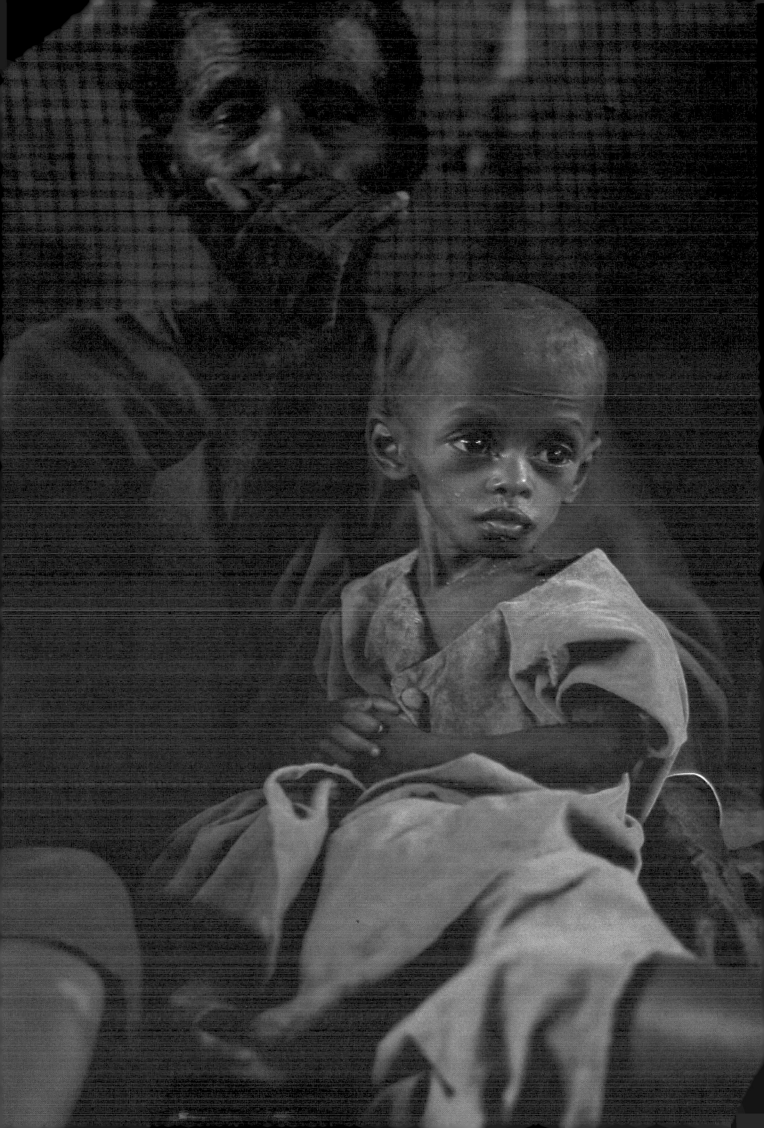

The camp at Korem

It was 6 am. A chill dawn crept over the mountains that glowered all around the vast plateau of Korem. The growing light revealed a layer of mist, white and impenetrable and as distinct as a geological stratum, over the plains. The coldness, the local people called it. It hung like a judgement over Ethiopia's largest refugee camp.

The new day stole across the serried lines of tents, uncovering a tableau of indignity, suffering and wretched resignation that the darkness had disguised. There were almost 1000 tents there, improvized from sticks and large plastic sheets and erected over pits dug two feet down into the hard black earth that was once prime crop-growing land. On average 40 men, women and children lived packed into each one; the proximity helped to preserve their body warmth. These were the lucky ones; many others had no shelter at all.

With the start of another day the refugees shook themselves into movement. In their open-ended dwellings they shivered as they removed the blankets and thick shammas that had protected them from the sub-zero temperatures of the highland night. They bared their pitiful sagging skin for a few moments as they donned thinner white garments which later in the day would deflect some of the anger of the hostile sun.

In the distance the funeral parties could be seen. Nine people had died in the night. Only nine. There was a time when more than 100 died every day in Korem, but that was in October 1984 when thousands of starving and diseased peasant farmers arrived every day, many of them beyond help. Now Korem was no longer a place of crisis but of dogged drudgery and hopeless survival. There were no farmers here any more; they had become camp dwellers who seemed to have forgotten everything except how to struggle through another day. Many of them had been here for ten months, some longer. Nine deaths were just part of the new reality that was camp life.

Waiting was what happened at Korem: waiting for the clinic to open, waiting for admission to the feeding programme, waiting for attention in the crowded hospital sheds, waiting for the preparation of the high-energy food for the badly malnourished, waiting for the government distribution of food which did not come yesterday, does not come today and probably will not come tomorrow.

Everywhere there were queues or else great herds of people, penned inside black plastic fences designed to bring some order to the milling chaos of bodies. Between the corrugated-iron hospital sheds they sat and waited, sometimes glancing up with a feeble curiosity as relief workers moved purposefully by. In their tents they sat and waited, their features washed by blank indifference. In desultory groups across the unsheltered plains they sat and waited for the temporary release of food or the permanent one of death.

Outside one tent crouched Aberbe Gabru. There was grey in the tight curls of his dark hair and his beard was grizzled, but he did not look the 70 years he claimed. They are hardy, these mountain people, and once they have passed the age of five, below which half the children die, they can in normal times live to a good age. Before him Gabru had five scrappy bundles of wood. He squatted on his haunches on the hard ground and surveyed them.

"What are these for?" the interpreter asked him. The old man looked mystified as the question was translated.

"They are firewood."

"Where did he get them?"

"From the hills."

"How long did it take him?"

"Two days. Every time he goes for firewood he must walk further."

"Where did he sleep last night?"

"Between the rocks, in the hills."

"What will he do with them now? Use them or sell them?"

The old man made no reply but looked up at the visitors and then at the pathetic piles of sticks. The message was quite clear. Only a visitor could afford to buy firewood, although a visitor, of course, would have no use for them. The two tattered and disgustingly soiled banknotes which he was given seemed impregnated with the misery of his entire nation. He was elated. The two birr would buy him enough grain, even at the grossly inflated

prices of Korem market, to last him with frugal use for a couple of months. In the bar at the Addis Hilton they would not have bought a glass of beer.

At 9 am the expatriate relief workers from the Save the Children Fund and doctors and nurses from the French organization Médecins Sans Frontières arrived from their ramshackle hotels in the town. They listened to the reports of the local people they employed as field workers in the camp. The news was that there would, that day, not be enough food to give their 7520 badly malnourished

Waiting for food, Alomata.

children the six daily meals they needed for recovery. Two meals would have to be omitted, the local SCF co-ordinator, Ato Fekadu, reported.

The nightwatchmen in the hospital wards, who all wore, almost as a badge of office, grotesque floral kipper-ties, fashionable imports from the time when the Emperor Haile Selassie kept Ethiopia in communion with the West, reported to the medics on who had died and who had been badly ill in the night.

Dr Serge Bechet was not long out of medical school. Like all the French medics, he was in his late 20s; the career structure for doctors in France is such that the only time they can easily volunteer for third-world service is between college and their first job. Korem was a baptism of blood: the patients and the problems were so many.

The young doctor shrugged. "There is only one problem here, starvation. People are dying of dysentery, pneumonia, typhus and relapsing fever, but what they really die of is hunger. The average weight of an adult here is 34 kilos, half the weight of a healthy person. What we need is more food. We are discharging people when they get better and then they go out and get no food and become ill again."

In the Save the Children Fund centre, the charity's field director, Kathy Bogan, was briefing her staff before she left on a two-day visit to the SCF camp in Kobbo and the towns of Kombolcha and Dese, the sites of the massive provincial warehouses that stored the grain brought in from the port of Assab, where aid was unloaded. Although the reports were that the warehouses were full, grain had not been reaching Korem in sufficient quantities for the past six weeks. Kathy Bogan wanted to know why.

The Save the Children Fund had six fully trained nutritionists in the camp, along with 50 Ethiopian auxiliaries and 120 peasants recruited in a food-for-work programme which offered grain in return for help in the camp's gigantic kitchens. As Kathy set out, her team began their daily tasks. That day in Korem there were about 100 newcomers, just arrived from the outlying countryside and most of them in dreadful condition. They had to be weighed and measured to determine their exact degree of malnutrition and then allocated to one of three feeding programmes. After that had been done there were now 742 children in the category of up to 20 per cent underweight who needed "supplementary feeding"; that meant an extra 500 grams of rice porridge and a quarter of a bread pancake called "kitta", all cooked in massive pans in the camp kitchen, and an extra two high-protein biscuits. In the category of between 20 and 30 per cent underweight, which in the relativity of starvation is classified as "moderately malnourished", there were now 5815 little specimens of skin and bone; they should have received intensive feeding of six high-energy drinks made up of soya wheat flour, butter oil, dried skimmed milk, sugar and boiled water, plus two meals each of biscuits, porridge and kitta. In the category of more than 30 per cent underweight — "critically malnourished" — were now 963 children who needed the same as those in intensive feeding plus six extra helpings of the drink.

This is what they should have received. But supplies had been severed by the Ethiopian Government, which claimed a transport shortage. Many relief workers, however, suspected that the stoppage was a deliberate attempt to starve peasants into "volunteering" for the Dergue's controversial resettlement scheme. Either way the result was that, on that one day in Korem, 6778 children would receive four tiny meals instead of the six their frail bodies needed. There were some who were too ill to care; 87 were being fed through the nose with gastric drips.

After being placed in one of the three categories the newcomers crossed to the de-lousing unit where their clothes were steamed for 20 minutes in old oil drums, their skin treated and their hair shaved. "Many people find it shameful but it has to be done," said the Ethiopian worker at the door of the roofless tent. In these highlands head shaving has many cultural implications. Western visitors were not encouraged to go in and watch.

Back at the hospital, a young Belgian midwife, Ines Huberty, was busy in the maternity ward. She worked in jeans and a T-shirt, her long, curly hair uncombed. She had already delivered four babies that morning. "Life goes on, even here," she said. "Besides, the birth of a new child is one of their few happinesses. Most women have already lost so many."

She worked with a matter-of-fact speed, interrupted by the odd burst of affection as she lifted one of the shrivelled infants and planted a kiss on its forehead. At that moment she was crouching over what looked like a new-born baby, though it was in fact eight months old.

"Her name is Hada. She was completely malnourished when she arrived three months ago and she had bronchial pneumonia. Now she takes on some weight and then gets diarrhoea and loses it. I am trying to fix an intravenous unit to rehydrate her, but I can't find a vein big enough to put the needle in. She is too small. Look."

The little girl's bulbous head, her arms, her legs, were covered with veins raised and bruised by the nurse's attempts. Finally she shifted a silver foil package that was getting in the way and successfully fixed the drip in the child's fragile arm, no thicker than a man's index finger.

What was in the package?

"A baby."

She opened the foil to reveal a tiny, tiny human being.

"It will die. It is too small, it came very early. In Europe it would be in an incubator, in Africa it will die."

It was past midday now, the seventh hour as the highlanders called it, using a clock that had not changed since biblical times. The relief workers returned to their hotel for lunch under a canvas awning. The French medics ate tinned paté, tuna fish, salami with rice, and a salad of tinned beans and tomatoes.

"Trust the French to eat well, even here," a visitor remarked with good humour.

"What do you expect?" replied a pretty French nurse, detecting an unintended accusation in the comment. "If we ate as the people do we should weaken, catch the illnesses, and be of no use to anyone."

Back at the camp Ato Fekadu was organizing the sorting of the food for the next day's cooking. In the compounds groups of two or three thousand people were sitting in rows, waiting patiently, placidly, with more hope than expectation, for they knew there would not be enough food to go around. There never was. Still they sat there ignoring the fact that at the transit camp a mile down the road they would be given two cooked meals a day if they went to volunteer for resettlement in the southwest of the country.

In the children's ward a young Frenchwoman with the worried smile of an earnest sixth-former was looking at a two-year-old child. Dr Valerie Schwoebel was in fact 29 and a fully qualified paediatrician. She was talking to a nurse about the child. "She is much better. She is doing fine."

"This little girl is called Sege. I have to confess that she is one of my favourites. When she arrived, months ago, she was badly starved and we fed her up. Three weeks ago she developed measles and we got her through that. Then, three days ago, she developed pneumonia; weak children often do after measles. I had to use an aspirator to remove fluid that had accumulated in her lungs but I think she will be OK."

She bent down and touched the sleeping child gently on the head. It was a gesture of love. The doctor smiled. She did not know that the next morning she would stare in disbelief at an empty bed. Sege was to die that night.

The Government's chief official with the local office of the Relief and Rehabilitation Commission was wandering through the camp on a tour of inspection. Yeshitila Demerraw was kind and genial, but cowed by the weasel-faced party man who dogged his every step.

"There is no food. There is none in the warehouses," Yeshitila said.

Yet United Nations officials who had just completed a survey said that the warehouses nearest to Korem were full to the ceiling. Yeshitila seemed genuinely perplexed to hear this.

"I did not know that. I had not been told. In any case we have no transport. We have only one lorry. You will have seen it broken down on the mountain road."

But Colonel Mengistu, the Ethiopian leader, had promised that army trucks would be used to move food now.

Yeshitila looked worried: "I have not been told that. People do not tell me these things. I just have to do the best I can."

He seemed to be doing that. As he walked he came across four women and a man who sat in a half-circle, moaning as

Right **Mother and child, Alomata.**
Overleaf **The camp at Korem, Wollo province, Ethiopia.**

they rocked back and forth, intoning some wailing litany.

"It is a funeral," he explained. "They are telling of the qualities of the life of the woman who died and was buried this morning."

He stopped and stood before the chief mourner and looked on, a silent but brutal interruption. She was a small woman, strikingly beautiful, with the fine-sculpted features of the Abyssinian highlander. Her ears were pierced, but now they were bare of the jewellery that had been in her family for generations. It was the last thing to go, but it had been sold that morning to buy the swaddling bands for the burial. She looked up at Yeshitila. There were tears in her eyes, but no accusation.

"Who has died?"

"Her sister," translated the RRC man.

"Where was she buried?"

"In the Coptic cemetery, over the plains. We have offered them a burial ground here but still, even in this condition, they prefer to walk for two hours to the churchyard."

All the women were looking up at him now. One of them had a growth the size of a large grapefruit in her throat, the result of an iodine deficiency. The appalling goitre held the gaze like a magnet.

"What did she die of?"

"The illness, in the stomach."

"When did she last eat?"

"Not for a long time."

"When did she last receive a food ration from the Government?"

Yeshitila translated the question into Amharic. He knew the shortcomings of his own Government and did not fudge the answer.

"Six weeks ago."

"Thank you."

He bowed with stiff dignity to the woman, to her companions, to the man, and walked away. The sun was being swallowed by another land beyond the mountains. Dusk falls quickly as a curtain in these highlands. As the gloom descended, the rocking orisons of the mourners rose again into the air and mingled with the blue smoke of a thousand tiny fires. Soon the coldness would be on the camp once more.

That was just one day in hundreds in the life of Korem. It was a day in January 1985, the month that Bob Geldof first arrived in Ethiopia with the £8 million profits of that first Christmas record, "Feed the World". Then he saw that £8 million was not enough. He went home and organized the Live Aid concerts. Now it was October, nine months later, and Geldof was to go to Korem to see how things had altered.

The first changes were apparent even before the Band Aid party climbed into the helicopter which one of the relief agencies had provided. The corner of Addis Ababa's Bole Airport, which had in January held only two British Hercules transport planes and a couple of RAF

tents, was now alive with activity. The British presence was now expanded and alongside it were the ops rooms of the Luftwaffe, filled with German air crew in their bright orange flying suits. All around were stacks of food being packaged on pallets in preparation for the airdrops which in January were only at an experimental stage but which had now become essential to the airborne relief effort. Between the sacks, groups of Ethiopian airport workers busied themselves with preparing more. The thunder of four huge engines battered their ears as one of

the Hercs prepared for take-off. Only the Russian Antonovs were, as before, silent; they stood on the far side of the apron with no sign of activity. But the day before, the European airmen said, they had flown in with hundreds of Ethiopian troops injured in the escalating war with the Eritreans. They also fly in the peasants from the north and offload them into trucks as part of the Dergue's resettlement programme.

The rains had been over for only a few weeks and, as the helicopter skimmed across the gentle hills which surround the capital, Geldof looked down from the co-

pilot's seat onto a different world. Places that had been brown and dry last time he saw this countryside were now bright yellow-green with the colour of new growth. The fields were patched with sections of gold where some early crops were already ripe for harvesting. The lakes were full. Flocks of pink flamingoes, in fluttering curves, swept up from them towards the aircraft windows.

"This country is beautiful," Geldof shouted, with genuine surprise, across the roar of the rotor blades. The pilot nodded.

The further north we flew the higher the plateau rose beneath us. It was a disconcerting experience. The 7000 foot plateau is heavily dissected by deep valleys and their trickling rivers which turn to tumultuous torrents for these few weeks after the rains. At one moment the aircraft would be skimming the grey-roofed tukuls of thick dry straw and mud; the next the ground would be stolen away, and we'd be 5000 feet above the floor of a massive canyon. From this vantage point it was easy to see how it was possible for a man to walk for ten days in these highlands and never come across a road.

A guided tour, Korem. *Overleaf* **Inmates of Korem.**

"I was flying this way three months ago when I heard a strange story," the pilot said over a crackling intercom. "I was delivering food to some remote villages when I was told of a community of monks who needed help at the bottom of one of these ravines. Would you like to go down and see what I found?"

Geldof nodded. The aircraft dropped suddenly onto its side and wheeled downwards to the edge of one of the canyons.

"I'll have to drop half of you at the top and then go down light. It's fairly tricky," said the pilot as he set the aircraft down. "I'll come back for the rest in a few minutes."

The sheer drop from the edge of the ravine was more than 2000 feet. At that point the cliff was broken by a sloping ledge about 100 yards wide before dropping steeply once again to the narrow, cutting river 1000 feet further below. On that ledge below was the monastery of Ganamba and the little village which surrounded it.

It was here on the top of the plateau three months before that the pilot had been told of the place. There were 38 monks in it and they were starving to death. In good times they lived by making pottery and bartering it for food with their neighbours, but now the villagers had nothing to give. They themselves were starving. The hilltop peasants had suggested that the food be left with them; someone from the monastery would climb to fetch it. But the pilot, from this height, could not discern any human life below and suspected the hilltop people had invented the story to gain extra rations. So he flew down and perched perilously on the ledge. Now he had brought us to do the same, but the manoeuvre was hazardous so we went in two loads. Geldof was in the first. The helicopter wheeled in a tight spiral down into the deep ravine.

The place was a green Eden now, though it must have been parched and dusty when first the helicopter landed there. The villagers, about two score of them, small people with soft curly hair and delicate features, dressed in ochre-coloured robes the texture of old sacking, came out of their huts to greet us. They put their hands together around ours in a gesture of prayerful salutation and after a multiplicity of double-bowed greetings, stood with us to watch the giant insect's take-off. Standing there waiting for it to return with the others, Geldof tried to imagine what, on that very first occasion, the villagers must have thought of the visitation of this angry beast which now had become a symbol of benison and hope.

The landing manoeuvres for today's visit were more perilous than ever before. On its previous monthly visits, as well as food it had brought one and a half tons of seeds; now the ledge was covered with ripening sorghum and barley. The helicopter had to set down in a tiny field where the early barley had already been harvested.

The monks lived at the far end of the rock shelf. We made our way along narrow paths chiselled into the side of the valley. There was not room for two people to pass and the women, with their short tousled hair and demure smiles, who traversed the mountainside carrying broad earthenware pots before them in both hands, moved off the track and picked their way delicately through the barley at our approach.

There was nothing grand about the monastery. It was merely another collection of dry grass huts surrounded by a pallisade of wattle and daub. Yet this was a special place, one of the repositories of the most ancient form of Christianity.

"Encompassed on all sides by the enemies of their religion, the Aethiopians

Above **Children of Korem watch the Geldof party arrive.** *Right* **Father and son, Korem.**

slept near a thousand years, forgetful of the world by whom they were forgotten," wrote Edward Gibbon in his *Decline and Fall of the Roman Empire*. For in the centuries when Christianity in the Western world was adapting to changing times, in the Abyssinian highlands, surrounded by nations dominated by Islam, it remained exactly as it was when it was first brought to the Axumite kingdom in the 4th century. There it persists, an archaic faith which forms a bridge between the ways of Judaism and Christendom, with its emphasis upon the Law and the Prophets and recognizing no Christian developments after the Council of Ephesus in 431 AD.

One of Geldof's passions is for antiques. Inside the monastery, he had been told, the Bible would be written in the antique language of Ge'ez, now dead in Africa as Latin is in Europe. The wood-bound books themselves would be hand-written on parchment in the Amharic script which, with its 321 syllables, is found only in Ethiopia; they would be highly decorated by the monks themselves or by their brethren in some greater monastic house. They would include unique Ethiopic liturgical texts and deutercanonical books of the Old Testament long since lost to both Christians and Jews in the outside world—the Books of Enoch, Jubilees, Judith, Tobit and the "Shepherd" of Hermas—and would contain arcane and secret traditions relating to circumcision, magical practices and prayers, and bapt-

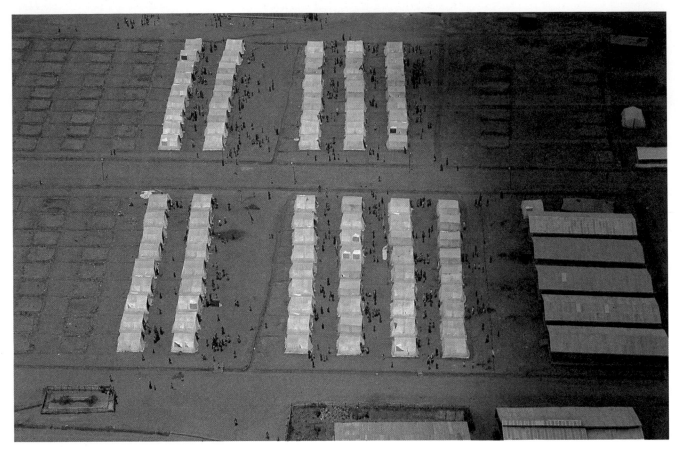

isms of threefold immersion. The monastery would have its own "tabot", a copy of the Ark of the Covenant which the Ethiopic Christians believe was brought from Jerusalem by Menelik, the son of the Queen of Sheba, to the ancient town of Axum, where today it rests in a special chapel guarded and seen only by an old and especially holy monk who, with his dying words, will nominate his successor.

But Ganamba was not to yield its secrets to Geldof that day. It was the Sabbath and entry was forbidden. By a postern gate one of the villagers went inside. Five minutes later he returned with an array of thick black pots, drinking bowls and lacquered chalices. Geldof wanted to buy, partly to boost the monkish economy but mainly because they were such queer and beautiful objects. But when he and the rest of the party had made their selection and offered to pay, the villagers told us we did not understand. These were gifts, all of them.

"You have given us food, seeds and tools. This is our gift to you," said the headman. Geldof tried to insist but it was clear that if the matter was pressed the people of Ganamba would be insulted.

They would not let us carry the pots to the aircraft. That would have been a discourtesy to us as guests, the headman explained. His people bore the gifts behind us. One chalice was filled with a sour millet beer and passed around. Then we climbed aboard and the gifts were handed in with simple ceremony.

So too was a pot of wild honey.

No, we insisted, we could not take food from there.

"It is our gift," said the headman. "Without you we would have nothing."

They stood on a little hillock, the entire lay population of Ganamba, and waved as the helicopter rose into the sky and up the side of the steep cliff. Geldof sat, with his precious little black pot wedged tightly between his knees, and waved back, silenced by the thanksgiving.

The helicopter headed north. Slowly the countryside was changing. We were nearing Korem, the start of it all, and the ground beneath us was turning brown and dry. The wind blew great swirling clouds of fine soil across the plains in the far distance. On the horizon dust-devils danced their fiendish little celebrations of the dryness.

Before the final rise of the mountains to Korem's high plateau, the little garrison town of Alomata lies. It is the site of a massive feeding centre run by World Vision and Mother Teresa's Sisters of Charity. From the air it looked dramatic. We decided to make a detour and stop there first.

Here in January an unhappy doctor could be seen on a daily tour of the lines of children hoping to be admitted to the scheme. There would be around 500 every day in eight separate lines from which the physician would choose as many as he had places available. Sometimes he would be able to pick as few as 20, for although there were 10,000 places in the centre they were all full, and children were only rarely discharged.

"The children are not in such bad shape now. They don't slip backwards as easily as they did," Geldof was told by the centre's technical manager, Nancy Sandberg, as she showed him around the long

Harbo camp, Wollo province, Ethiopia, is shrinking. At the height of the famine it housed 5000 people. Only 99 tents remain. *Right and overleaf* The sick bay, Harbo camp hospital.

feeding sheds. The last feed of the day was over and the children, with their mothers, were sitting in rows and singing.

"We wash our hands before we eat, before we eat, before we eat," they chanted to a jerky tune with a lot of clapping.

It was a different song in every shed, a local Ethiopian worker told Geldof. There were songs for fever, songs for malaria, songs for diarrhoea.

The sights in the feeding centre's hospital were as shocking as ever, but where before there had been hundreds of skeletal children on the point of death now were only dozens.

"Only dozens," said Geldof, with heavy irony.

"The depressing thing is that we have given the people seeds to plant and food to eat while they waited for the harvest. But the rains have failed again so there will be no harvest. As well as the 8000 children we have in special feeding, we have been giving out dry rations for 70,000 people. The lack of harvest means that we will have to feed those 70,000 for another 12 months. And the number is growing constantly," said Nancy, who after a year in Alomata was beginning to look very weary.

As the Band Aid team prepared to leave, a battered old landrover came hurtling through the town. It screeched to a halt and out jumped Michael Buerk of BBC Television, Mike Wooldridge of BBC

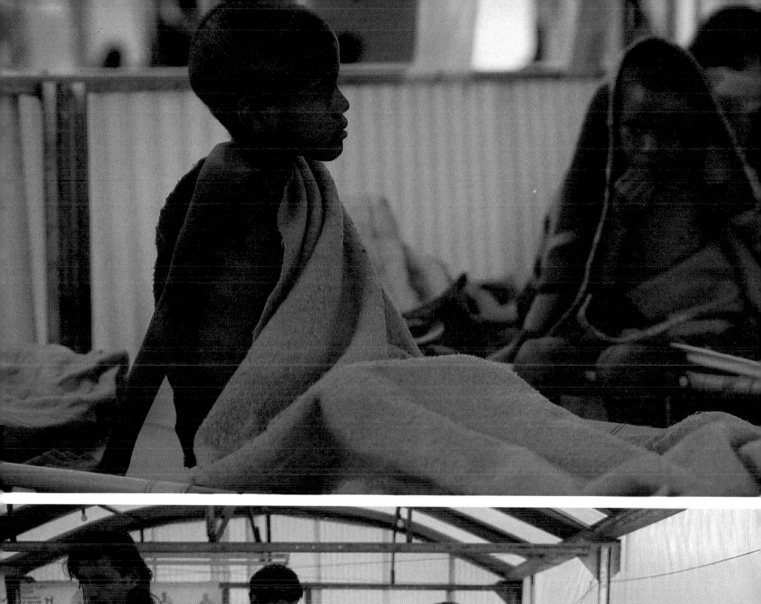

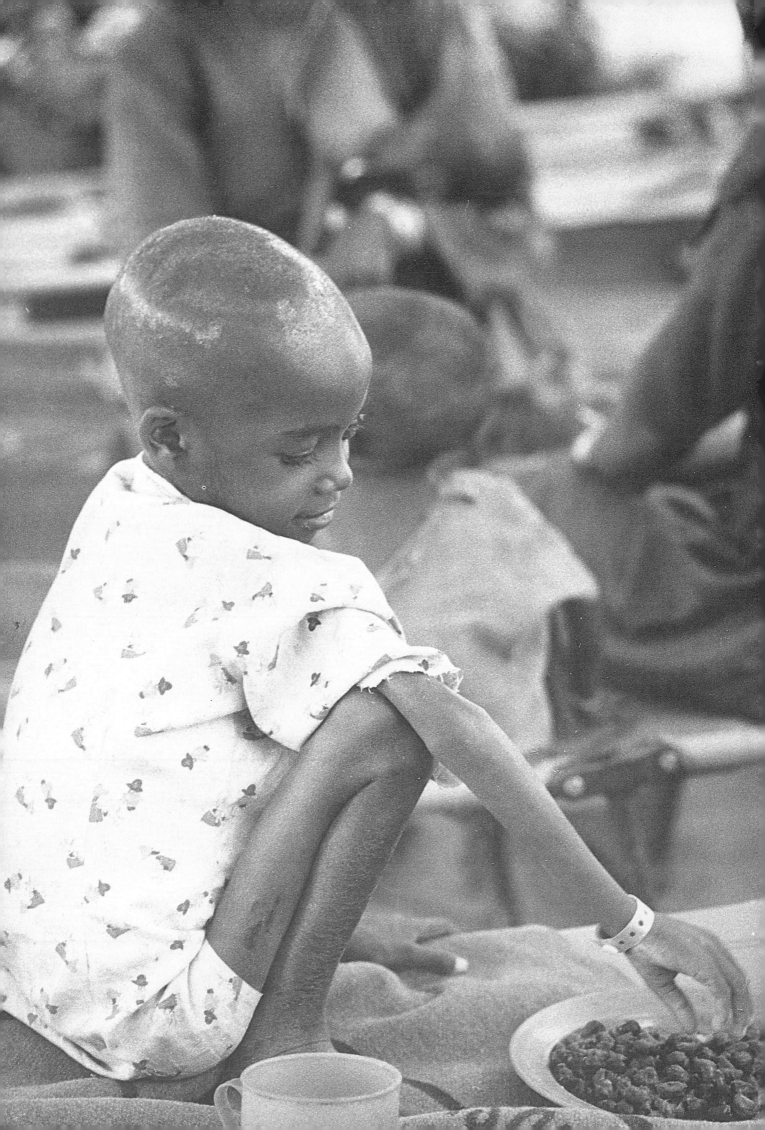

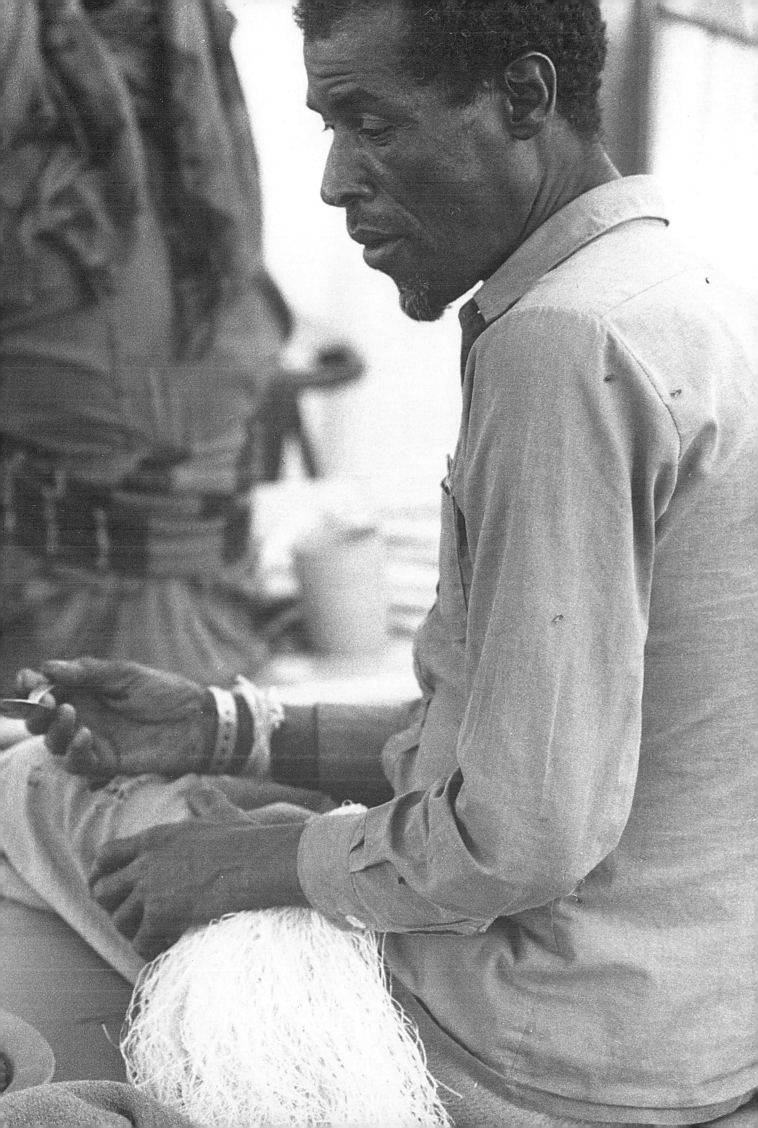

Radio and Mohammed Amin, the Visnews cameraman. This was the trio who had first reported the horror of Korem camp, exactly one year before.

"It's great to see you," said Buerk.

"It's good to see you," said Geldof. "Your film was the reason I got involved in all this in the first place."

But it was not Geldof they were pleased to see so much as the BBC film crew which accompanied him.

"Our camera's knackered," said Buerk. "You'll have to give us yours. We're here to do a film on Korem, one year on."

Geldof's helicopter was circling over Korem while Buerk and Co. were still in their landrover rattling up the long switchback of perilous roads between Alomata and Korem, with Mohammed Amin's camera now fixed by Tim Rex, who was an engineer before he became a video recordist. The aircraft circled the camp twice, looking for a good place to land.

Even from the air the differences were apparent. A year before, there had been around 85,000 people here. Now there was a chequerboard of patches where once there had been tents; the place was perhaps half its former size. The helicopter came down in a space between the de-lousing sheds and the SCF feeding centre. Even before the rotor had stopped turning, the aircraft was surrounded by a crowd of about 3000 excited children.

"Ferenji, ferenji," they shouted in a great chorus. The word, in Amharic, means foreigner. The cry follows any new white face in Korem so constantly that it becomes, like the noise of the cicadas elsewhere in the continent, something which blends into the visitor's unconscious memory of the place.

To say that the children looked healthy would be misleading. By European standards they were scrawny and undernourished; by African standards they were in the bloom of health. Their upper arms were fleshy. Their thighs were strong. They surrounded Geldof in a gigantic chanting circle. The adults who stood among them had been made by food aid to look comparatively fit and healthy too.

Geldof spent his first 15 minutes in Korem not looking around but answering, to camera, a series of inane questions for an American television station concerned with the pseudo-philosophical implications of pop music as a vehicle for social change. In the background the children of Korem flocked, as they always do, to a white face in the hope of receiving something. A clearer example of the contrast between the world of pop in which he lived and the world of starvation in which he now found himself would have been hard to find.

"Of course it's crap," said Geldof afterwards, when taxed with the incongruity. "But if it helps raise money then you have to put up with the crap. For God's sake,

look what these people have to put up with."

One year after the BBC film, despite the improved health of the people, there was something even more depressing and squalid about Korem. There were no longer more than 100 people dying every day. There were no longer the huge, unmanageable masses of humanity which once crowded the plains. There were no longer the same problems about getting food up the steep and serpentine roads onto the plateau. But paradoxically now, more than ever before, Korem was a sump of human degradation.

As Geldof wandered between the rows of tents and buildings, with his crowd of chanting children, the feeling became oppressive. The passageways between the long hospital sheds of corrugated iron had always been collecting places for ordure and detritus; of course, there were always orderlies to clear it away, but now it seemed that whatever the cleaners did the filth was ingrained in the place. It was now more than squalid, it was sordid. The feculence had become institutionalized. Buildings which, when newly erected at the beginning of the year, had seemed quite acceptable as a temporary solution to the overwhelming problems of so many people had now taken on an unacceptable air of permanence.

One or two attempts had been made to grow sorghum at the edge of the camp, and a pitiful cluster of vermilion flowers had been planted by the entrance to one of the feeding centres, but in the main there was no feeling of useful employment or even of hope about the place. There were in fact fewer people here than there had seemed to be from the air. The population was now down to about 23,000, but that seemed to have done nothing to improve the atmosphere. Though, after months of food aid, the refugees had lost the dreadful listlessness of malnutrition, it had been replaced with the apathy of people whose lives have lost all natural rhythm and, it seemed at times, all sense of purpose. The adults sat, like bored Western teenagers, and stared truculently into the distance.

The children mobbed Geldof and his party and begged with an aggressiveness which was both new and alarming. The criss-cross of paths which had been worn deep and hard between the ranks of dirty tents formed a net which seemed to have a psychological counterpart. Some of these people had now been in Korem for almost two years. They had forgotten their old way of life and showed no sign of wanting to find a new one. It had been replaced by a macabre kind of resignation.

The policy of the Ethiopian Government is now to dismantle camps, or at least turn them into emergency centres where badly malnourished people can be given therapeutic courses of feeding and then, when well, be sent home. The model camp in this respect is the one run by the Irish charity Concern at Harbo to the south of

Korem, which the Band Aid team also visited that day. It has a population of only 1400 and a turnover time of only three or four weeks per inmate.

But Korem is too big to be transformed in this way. A few weeks before Geldof arrived, the Government had tried to cut down the numbers by sending 11,000 of the inmates back to their homes with the promise of dry ration distribution at centres nearer their villages. The week after Geldof left, aid workers were expecting to begin the process of screening 10,000 more refugees to make sure they were fit to be sent back to their homes in the Sekota area, 40 miles to the west, which the Government had recently recaptured from the rebel guerillas.

It was difficult, Geldof said, to see what alternative there was to such a move. The Ethiopian Government seemed to agree. Two days after our visit, when Geldof had flown back to London and on to Strasbourg to address the European Parliament, a convoy of lorries arrived in Korem. Men with sticks, with armed soldiers from the town's garrison in the background, rounded up 600 refugees and herded them like cattle into trucks, not to be returned to their homes in Sekota, but to be forced on the long journey south to compulsory resettlement. The operation was conducted so brutally that a full 10,000 of the camp's population took fright and fled into the surrounding hills. Most hid there for only a few days before returning. The desolation of those utterly barren highlands was such that even Korem was preferable, though some were so afraid that they never returned. For Geldof it was to prove a depressing epilogue to his tour of the continent.

Not that he was anything other than dispirited when he left Korem. Before he climbed aboard the helicopter for the final time he turned and surveyed the camp where, for him at least, this exhausting African odyssey had had its beginning.

"No human being should be forced to live in circumstances like this," he said. "It is not enough for us to have kept them from dying if this is how we leave them to exist. We have helped to save their lives. Now we must give them a life worth living."

It was something which Geldof had said, often, before. On the stage with Live Aid it had had a fine rhetorical ring. On the windswept plains of Korem it echoed only with a bleak desperation. Geldof now knew it wasn't as simple as that.

Right Geldof and Jenden pick their way through a bog at Korem. *Overleaf* Leaving: the helicopter takes off.

Spending Band Aid money

So what did the trip across Africa achieve? It recharged the batteries for both Jenden and Geldof, at no cost to the Band Aid fund. In the hectic round of fund raising in Britain, Europe and America they had begun to feel removed from the real cause and purpose of Band Aid: the famine in Africa. And for both of them the trip brought good news and bad news.

The good news was that aid can work. They saw projects throughout the Sahel, Sudan and Ethiopia that would not be there if international relief and Band Aid money had not been given. They saw many people who would not be alive without the help of the rest of the world. The high point for both of them was Port Sudan on the Sudanese coast towards the end of the trip. Our BA 125 swooped down on the desert from 10,000 feet and dune-hopped towards a line of trucks waiting to go through the Port Sudan immigration and police checkpoint. The BBC filmed through the window and Geldof took snapshots. Band Aid had been criticized by the BBC programme *Panorama* for buying lorries that were derelict and incapable of carrying goods through the desert. A team of engineers and mechanics had been working on them for a month. Now, they were moving towards Khartoum carrying relief aid.

Chris Morris of the BBC asked Geldof for a quote.

"OK," he said. "Sod *Panorama*."

The bad news was that countless thousands of people were still starving and suffering. Sometimes the enormity of the problem was overwhelming. Nobody can stop the Sahara desert moving 20 miles every year, swamping towns and fertile land. But near Timbuctoo, which has been overrun by the desert, they saw a small

project for planting rice that has made enough money to feed the entire population of the town for the past year of drought. Nobody can stop the civil war and deprivation in Chad, but a bridge which Band Aid intends to build over a tributary of the Chari River will bring food and medicine to thousands of people. It will help to alleviate the misery.

The main aim of the trip was to get publicity, to show the people at home that the famine has affected parts of the world which many barely know exist: Mali, Burkina Faso, Niger and Chad, places where Band Aid had so far invested no money. Both Geldof and Jenden feel this aim was achieved, through the nightly broadcasts on the BBC (of film which was also shown on ITV and NBC in America) and the articles in *The Times* and *The Sunday Times*. They hope it will be furthered by this book. Whether this publicity translates into more donations for famine relief is yet to be seen, but aid experts

Above **The London end of Live Aid.**
Right **One of the scenes that inspired the whole event: Ethiopia, October 1984. Picture: John Reardon.**

believe there is a strong correlation between the amount donated and the publicity the famine receives.

At the time of writing, two weeks after the trip, the practical results are beginning to emerge. Band Aid has so far received proposals for 160 projects in the Sahel, Sudan and Ethiopia. These projects have been submitted to experts from the Mustard Seed Development Group who log them on computer, evaluate them and note the areas and issues they deal with. They are then sent to the Band Aid advisory committee, ten people from institutions including Sussex and Reading Universities, the School of Oriental and African Studies and the School of Tropical Hygiene and Medicine in London and Georgetown University in Washington

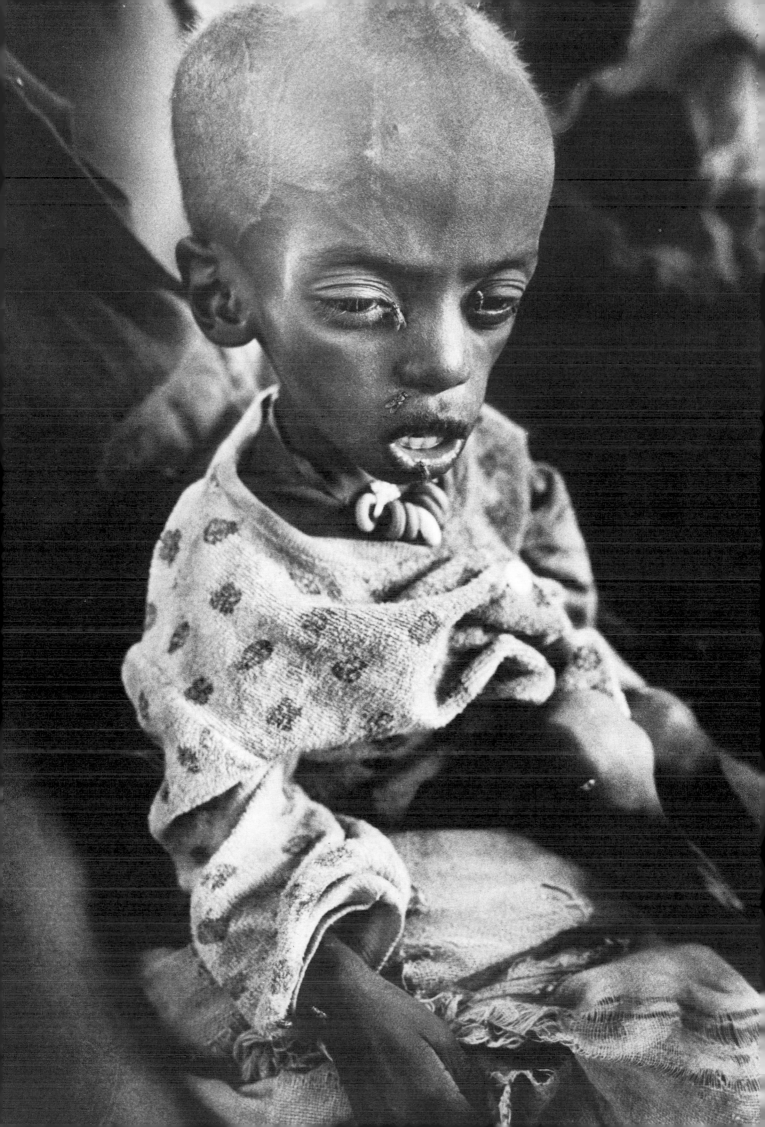

DC. When the advisory group decides it has enough information it makes its decision about which projects to support. Band Aid has already decided to build the bridge in Chad for $1.2 million and is processing a plan to send emergency aid to Mali, Chad, Niger and Burkina Faso.

So far in 1985 Band Aid has collected £54 million. Jenden believes this may rise to £70 million. It is a remarkable achievement for one organization. Only a year has passed since Geldof sat at home in Chelsea and watched the original BBC film by Michael Buerk from Korem. While other viewers sat horrified, Geldof decided to do something. The result was Band Aid and the song called "Feed the World". Geldof thought then that if he raised £70,000 he would be lucky. It raised £8 million. Then came the transatlantic concert, Live Aid, which raised record-breaking amounts.

The money will be broadly divided in the following way: 60 per cent for long-term projects, 20 per cent for continued emergency aid and famine relief and 20 per cent for shipping and transport.

Geldof said on the first day of the trip that if Band Aid had saved one life the money and the effort would have been worth it. It has saved many more than that. The greatest single reason for Band Aid's existence was given by a UNICEF field worker in Port Sudan. "I know that in Sudan alone Band Aid saved thousands of lives this year. They managed to get cholera vaccine to us quicker than any other agency. If they had not, these people would now be dead."

Band Aid's future is uncertain. Jenden told Geldof when he joined Band Aid that he would stay for six months. He has now been working almost full-time for the organization for a year. Geldof says that he never intended Band Aid to have a long life. "You can't keep getting on your horse and charging," he said during the trip. He intends to wind down his role in Band Aid after Christmas. He will remain chairman of the Board of Trustees and will spend at least a couple of days a week behind the scenes at Band Aid, but he now says that he wants to go back to music, to being a full-time Boomtown Rat.

"I never wanted Band Aid to become an institution. We raised the issue, the funds and the sympathy. When we finished, hopefully the emergency will be over. Then the real work begins. But at least no-one can now say: 'I didn't know'." One statistic shows the enormity of the famine and suffering that remains: all the £54 million that Band Aid has raised so far this year is only enough to keep the famine-stricken people of Sudan alive for seven weeks.

In the face of facts like that, Geldof has a simple response. He quotes his favourite line from the 18th-century philosopher Edmund Burke, who wrote: "Nobody made a greater mistake than he who did nothing because he could only do a little." This year has seen a lot of people put that into practice.

Band Aid money has bought for the famine victims of Africa:

17,000 tons	Grain
2,000 tons	Milk powder
1,200 tons	Sugar
1,200 tons	Vegetable oil
140 tons	Lentils
200 tons	Medical supplies and vitamins
29	Landrovers
18	Water tankers
169	Lorries
4	Mobile workshops
12	Land cruisers
10	Pick-ups
2	Bulldozers
200,000 gallons	Diesel fuel
52 tons	Plastic sheeting (reinforced)
41	Hospital tents
3	Clinics
200,000	Hand tools, picks and shovels
250,000	Feeding utensils
10 tons	Tarpaulin
15	Containers of clothing and cloth
10	Farm ploughs
150 tons	Seed
200,000	Blankets
3	Water-drilling rigs
40 tons	Water-pumping equipment
200 tons	High-energy biscuits
£1¼ million	Vehicle parts and tyres
1	Containerload of hospital equipment
1	Bridge
2	Vehicle compounds
£250,000	Seed, oxen and hand tools

The Band Aid fleet of nine ships has so far carried over 100,000 tons of aid to Africa, much of it for other agencies.

CHARITIES AND ORGANIZATIONS SERVED BY BAND AID

1 UNICEF Sudan
2 UNICEF Mozambique
3 UNICEF Ethiopia
4 Menschen für Menschen
5 CAFOD
6 UNDP Chad
7 War on Want
8 World Vision Germany
9 World Vision Great Britain
10 Oxfam
11 Norwegian Church Aid
12 Lutheran World Federation
13 CARE Sudan
14 Save the Children Fund USA
15 Ethiopian Orthodox Church
16 Norwegian Missionary Society
17 Catholic Relief Societies
18 South Ethiopian Synod
19 Evangelical Free Church of Norway
20 Interkerklijke Stichting Ethiopia
21 Christian Relief and Development Association
22 Hope Enterprise
23 MEDAR
24 Concern Dublin
25 Save the Children Fund UK
26 German Agency for Technical Co-ordination
27 British Red Cross Society
28 League of Red Cross Societies
29 League of Red Cross and Red Crescent Delegation
30 Ethiopian Red Cross Society
31 International Committee of the Red Cross
32 Sudan Council of Churches
33 EOC/DICAD
34 Relief Society of Tigre
35 Eritrean Relief Association
36 MTMTSC
37 Help the Aged
38 Oromo Relief Association
39 United Nations High Commission for Refugees
40 Wrexham Round Table Association
41 Presiding Bishop Fund for World Relief
42 Eritrean Relief Council
43 Feed the Children Ministries Ethiopia
44 Embassy of the Democratic Republic of Sudan
45 Third World Self-help Development Ireland
46 Canadian International Development Agency (CIDA)
47 Christian Outreach
48 Ockenden Venture
49 Irish African Friendship Committee
50 Ethiopian Government
51 Littleway Association
52 Relief and Rehabilitation Commission Ethiopia
53 Lambeth Women For Peace
54 Christian Aid London
55 Interkirk URK/EOC
56 British Air Reserve
57 Euro-Action Acord
58 International Medical Relief
59 A M International
60 You and Me Action for Third World
61 Commission for Refugees Sudan
62 Lifeline International
63 Leonard Cheshire Foundation
64 National Children's Commission
65 GOAL Ireland
66 ADRA Ireland
67 ADRA Holland
68 Swedish Philadelphia Church Mission
69 UNEOA
70 Verona Fathers
71 SOS Sahel International
72 Terre des Hommes
73 World Food Programme
74 Relief and Rehabilitation Commission Sudan
75 Médecins Sans Frontières
76 CARE Canada
77 Canadian Red Cross
78 Save the Children British Columbia
79 CPAR
80 Australian Council of Churches
81 Australian Baptist World Aid Relief Committee
82 Australian Catholic Relief
83 Australian Lutheran World Services
84 Churches Drought Action for Africa
85 Australian World Cross
86 World Vision Australia
87 Australian Freedom from Hunger Campaign
88 Community Aid Abroad
89 Austcare
90 Adventist Development Relief Agency of Australia
91 Save the Children Australia